The Writing Journey

Lessons From Nancy's Tutoring Corner

Nancy B. Velasco, MSEd
Education Specialist

The Writing Journey
Lessons From Nancy's Tutoring Corner

Published By

Nancy B. Velasco. MSEd – Publishing
PO Box 453
Brea, CA, 92822

Website: Https://NancyVelasco.com

Printed in the United States of America

Library of Congress Control Number: 2025904234

ISBN 978-1-966706-00-7 Paperback
ISBN 978-1-966706-01-4 eBook
ISBN 978-1-966706-03-8 Hardcover

Dedication

To Ada, Charlie, Mio, and Jacquelyn.

Enjoy the journey! Thank you for joining me on the adventure.

Table of Contents

Section I: From Journaling to Story Writing

Journaling, as you will soon learn, enthralls the heart, lightens the mind, and captures the senses in a rapturous sort of way. It provides a means for deeply assessing, sometimes dreaming, and certainly not merely getting caught up in the ordinary. Welcome to a magnificent adventure! I pass you the writing baton with great eagerness and look forward to narrating the journey.

Do not limit yourself to only

writing in the journal book when I

give such an instruction. Write,

write, and write some more —

everywhere you go!

Chapter 1 Getting Organized and Journaling

Chapter Objectives

- Organize journal entries using a table of contents.

- Create journal entries.

- Write journal entries using a sensory technique.

- Become more aware of your surroundings.

Welcome to our beautiful adventure. As my fingers begin to activate the keys, and the words appear on the screen before me, mentally the shape and content of this season in our lives--yours and mine --begins! As your narrator and mentor, I will start by expressing a joyful welcome! Thank you for joining me! Let's proceed!

Setting up the Table of Contents

Pick up your journal and favorite writing instrument. Should you not possess a nice journal, go shopping! This treasured writing piece will surely contain something worth holding onto for years to come. Pick out a journal that reflects something about yourself, your character, or things you love. While combing through office supplies or hobby shelves for your prized journal, also obtain some writing instruments:

pens, pencils, erasers, and page flags. These items will serve as our getting started supplies.

Before we dive deeply into the writing and learning jungle, take a moment to set up a Table of Contents. May I suggest this type of organization for the first or second page of the adventure journal:

Table of Contents

PAGE	DATE	TITLE/CONTENT

Next, number the pages of your new journal. Page numbers will enable you to quickly find writings of special memories and thoughts at a later point. It will provide easy access to rich highlights of our time together. Additionally, these pages will serve as a place to practice exercises and record your thoughts.

Get Ready to Write!

Listen Up!

Listen! Do you hear that? No, really, what do you hear? Answer this first question in your journal as we embark. This first journal entry will help with fine tuning listening skills. Also, it increases sensory writing abilities. Sit quietly now and listen to the sounds around you. Write about what you hear. Remember to log this first journal entry into the table of contents.

Journal Entry – (Today's Date) What do I hear?

Congratulations! You just created your first journal entry. Certainly, the "What do I hear?" responses will differ with each destination. As you change locations during the days ahead, consider adding more "What do I hear?" entries. Fine tuning ears to listen takes practice!

Get ready to add even more entries. The next one lies just ahead. Journal entries can include the ones mentioned in this book. Also, begin taking your journal with you. Writing ideas can arise in many different places. Create journal entries to capture such delightful thoughts! Fill the journal book with entries prompted by this adventure, but also ones you come up with spontaneously. Do not limit yourself to only writing in the journal book when I give such an instruction. Write, write, and write some more – everywhere you go!

Now Look!

Look! Do you see it? Okay, so we all know that hearing only gives us a partial perspective. Take time to answer this next question. What do you see? Carefully look around and write about what your eyes observe.

Journal Entry – (Today's Date) – What do I see?

Hopefully, this writing experience made you smile, brought a sense of peaceful contentment, and gave you an opportunity to test out writing descriptively. Continue to add more seeing and hearing journal entries as you go about your week. Now, let's liven up the stage, shall we?

Summary

As we step forward into deeper levels of writing, embrace an increased sense of awareness. Sensory writing requires such attention. Each sense adds a new dimension and broadens our perspective. The words will continue to flow like an ocean. As noted earlier, establishing a system for organizing it all begins by building a table of contents, adding progressive journal entries, and recording sequential page numbers. Keep writing!

Chapter Questions

1. Explain the benefits of beginning your journal with a table of contents.

2. Does careful listening improve your writing?

3. How does careful observation (seeing) help you become a better writer?

4. Plan for making the most of your writing journey. What supplies will you use? What do you still need to purchase? Who will you invite to join you on this writing journey?

No doubt, a new narrative book,

with you as the author, will soon

reach the hands and hearts of

people around you. Enjoy the

journey!

Chapter 2 Narrative Writing

Chapter Objectives

- Expand writing to include all five senses.

- Merge the five senses with the five Ws.

- Develop the art of adding in characters.

- Go beyond by including imaginative scenes.

- Write a narrative book.

Now, just for fun, look back at what you wrote in response to the questions, "What do I hear?" and "What do I see?" Yes, you heard and saw these things. Can you imagine having a character in a narrative type of story hearing or seeing these as well? For example, my personal journal entry noted the sounds of a noisy city. If I add a character, it might look and sound like the following:

Joyce Lee Graham sat looking out her bedroom window. She wondered if her mom would forgive her for the mean words spoken earlier that morning. The preteen frowned, sad over the circumstances which caused her to get grounded. As she sat, the noise of cars zooming by outside her window only made the girl want to escape even more.

The birds chirping and neighborhood kids laughing in the distance made her curiosity rise.

"Maybe if I wash the dishes after lunch, Mom will declare a pardon and set me free." The girl whispered, leaning back in her chair.

The sound of her mom chopping carrots and the smell of rich tomato soup filled the air. Joyce felt sorry for saying mean things to her mom. This, the lady that has taken such good care of her, had asked for help with the laundry chores. Complaining certainly created tension. Joey squealed and yelled out, breaking through the girl's sullen thoughts.

"Come on out for lunch now!" The four-year-old brother shouted as his feet pitter pattered back down the hallway.

Sensory Narrative Writing

Test out this idea! For your next journal entry, play with the sounds and sights noted in the first two entries, and add one or more characters. You can create a totally new character or maybe think of someone in one of your storybooks already in progress. Imagine a scene in which you weave in these sounds and sights? Test it out for your next journal entry.

Did you add characters? I really enjoy this type of imaginative writing. We only tested it out using our sense of hearing and seeing. What would happen if you wrote about all five senses? Perhaps move to a new location: a park, an airport, a different room at home, a shopping mall, or a basketball court. You decide where to sit! For this next journal entry, please include all five senses. Write down everything you see, hear, smell, taste, and feel. Enjoy the process!

Become more aware and begin writing a detailed descriptive explanation of your environment and how you respond to it. Routinely journal about the world around you and include all the sensory aspects. Train your mind in perceptivity. Content ideas for narrative stories will emerge. Continue to ask yourself, "What do I see? What do I hear? What do I smell? What do I feel? What do I taste?" Write your responses daily in different settings. Make sure to update the table of contents. These entries can prove invaluable in stirring creativity for writing an interesting story.

Journal Entry – (Today's Date) – All Five Senses – A New Spot

Can you add at least one character to the most recent location described? Use your imagination. Create a scene. Rewrite it now. Get used to rewriting. You may have sat under an educational schooling system that led you to believe or feel that rewriting something meant the first version proved unworthy – a failure. Think of it differently now. That first writing serves as the light coat of paint on a beautiful canvas. Each rewrite becomes a new layer to the unfolding pictorial masterpiece. Instead of that sigh feeling mounting within, replace it with that of a fluttering butterfly learning how to flap new wings and soar higher. You have been placed on this earth at this time in history to express the Creator's beauty – that crafted inside of you. Spread your writing wings and soar! Write again! Add people to your unfolding art.

Journal Entry – (Today's Date) – My Five Senses + Characters

The 5 Senses Meet the 5 Ws

Have you written at least one journal entry that contains all five senses? Did you add characters? Great! This next challenge will send your writing climbing higher! Do you remember the 5 Ws from elementary school?

- Where?
- When?

- Who?
- What?
- Why?

Take the merger challenge! Look at the journal writing you did that involved using the five senses. Next, can you add in, or rather merge to include, all 5 Ws? The first time trying this method may leave you with a Bambi like feeling. Do you remember Bambi, the baby deer who initially had very wobbly legs. Keep at it! Before long an entire story unfolds, and it changes the world! Test drive this one, then practice it daily for a month!

Create a new journal entry that contains all five senses. Describe a location – "the where." Now let your imagination assist you even more. Help the reader feel present at the scene.

Develop the story by describing the timing – the "when." If this scene depicts the winter season, add in snowflakes, mittens, a shovel, gloves, or other elements to provide hints of time. Maybe this scene takes place during an event, if so, add candles to the birthday cake, or fireworks to a national holiday celebration. Perhaps you can recall a historical event, placing the account in the middle of 1939 when WWII began. Consider speeding ahead and futuristically introducing the reader to Star Year 98745. You can even share the speed of time. The clock ticked slowly as the minutes passed.

Add in characters – the "who," and do so with flare. While different styles exist, I personally prefer a brief description of the lead character towards the beginning, then scatter hints of favorite clothing, personality traits, eye color, and inner thoughts, both good and bad, along the way. This helps the reader get acquainted with the character in a similar fashion as meeting a new friend or person in real life. Over time friendships develop. Individuals become better in tune with each other.

Include a nice action filled plot for the "what" portion of the scene. While my aging body no longer accommodates riding rollercoasters, plots work well with the rise and fall of action, with the climax, the protagonist saving the day at the peak of it all.

Teach a lesson, the overall "why" of the story. What do you wish readers to learn. Have the characters somehow overcome challenges to arrive with such insights and wisdom.

Journal Entry – (Today's Date) – The Unfolding Story

The Book Challenge

If you just finished the first round of combining everything, how many pages appeared? Did anything surprise you? Now, take the book challenge! Create a five senses journal entry each day for the next month. Keep changing the location as this will add more flavor. Afterwards, take your journal book, sit down at the keyboard, and if you have not already done so, add in the 5W's. No doubt, a new narrative book, with you as the author, will soon reach the hands and hearts of people around you. Enjoy the journey! Each location you journal about could spark a new narrative scene, a new chapter.

The Imagination Journey

In addition to asking the "What do I hear, see, taste, touch, smell questions," take it to the next level by using your imagination. Afterall, we cannot always go to the actual location of a desired narrative story scene. For this part, use your imagination! Use your mental imagery to help you prepare for writing. Do you see that volcano about to erupt? Pick an imaginary location. Next, populate it with sights, sounds, smells, tastes, and feelings. Now, write what you just mentally thought about. Your goal includes getting the reader to also see what you mentally saw.

For an interesting story, make sure to add in some rising action that includes conflict. Of course, teach a lesson along the way!

Journal Entry – (Today's Date) – What do I imagine?

Clearly, your imagination filled full of sensory elements can lead you to writing an entire storybook! Continue journaling and have fun! Remember to develop characters that pull at the heart of the readers. Double check to insure you included all 5Ws in each scene – meaning each chapter.

Summary

Continuing to assemble this writing collage challenges us to move beyond ink on a page. Engaging senses take on new heights and personality with the emerging dynamics of story characters. Telling our story with intentionality naturally leads to the presentation and layout of the 5Ws: where, when, who, what, and why. We will look at this in more detail in the next chapter. As you practice creating scenes and embedding characters, consider having some interactions. Describe how the people move. Have your characters engage in a dialogue. Can you imagine what a character says? Does the boy named Joshua raise his hands, kick the sand, or spit in the river? We will examine character emotions and expressions in the next chapter.

Chapter Questions

1. Make a list of locations that you could use for story settings. Can you think of real places to visit, observe, and journal about?

2. How does observing different locations help in creating a better story?

3. Look through the journal entries you wrote so far. Which phrases or sentences help the readers feel like they have come along with you on the journey?

4. Turn back to the example narrative of Joyce Lee Graham. How does adding a descriptive narrative help this story? Additionally, how does adding dialogue improve the storyline?

5. Narration versus dialogue: Explain how the narration helps you as the reader feel present in the location of the story. Explain how adding dialogue brings the character to life. Make a note of any other observations to contrast narration to dialogue.

6. How would you define sensory writing?

7. Of the five senses, which one do you like the most? Explain.

If your story contains scenes in which the characters learn that cheating on a test will earn them bad grades and that lying will get them suspended from school, you may decide to pick "honesty" as the theme.

Chapter 3 Completing the Story

Chapter Objectives

- Progress from the 5Ws to the more formal narrative word usage.

- Write a nice setting consisting of a description of time and location.

- Discover the loveliness of adding more descriptive language.

- Use the terms protagonist, antagonist, and narrator in identifying and developing characters.

- Experiment with developing characters in writing by including physical, emotional, positive, and negative attributes.

- Build an exciting plot by including an exposition (introduction), rising action, conflict, a climax, falling action, and a resolution.

- Make the story worthwhile by including at least one theme and a moral.

What makes for a most interesting read? So far, you have written spontaneous journal entries. These creatively flow from the heart. However, most writers find that the adventure weaved in one's inner being appears so wild that the reader could benefit from having a tour guide of sorts to assist with interpreting, walking ahead to direct the next step, and pointing out the exciting parts. Since such a guide will not appear each time for the reader, adding in more organization without destroying creativity goes next in our discussion. Much like layering a cake, we will focus on the main ingredients needed for a narrative story.

Laying Out the Pieces

Moving from earlier stages of writing necessitates becoming more aware and comfortable with different terminology. Take time to check your understanding and notice the connections between early elementary terms and other wordings, those used by students advancing in the skill of writing.

Early Terms
Where
When
Who
What
Why

Early writers become acquainted with the 5 Ws: where, when, who, what, and why. Additionally, teachers encourage students to include a hero, the good guy, and a villain, the bad one.

For simplicity's sake, these familiar 5 Ws continue to mentally stay in the mind of the writer even in later years. However, as the students increase in skills, these same 5 Ws transform. In working with many students, I have come across several young people, who for whatever reason, fail to see the connection between these earlier terms and the ones presented next.

Early Terms	Support Words	Later Terms	Support Words
Where		Setting	Location
When			Time
Who	Hero Villain	Characters	Protagonist Antagonist Narrator Protagonist supporters Antagonist supporters Others
What		Plot	Exposition Rising Action (Include Conflict) Climax Falling Action Resolution
Why		Themes (categories for the morals)	Morals (lessons to learn)

Look closely and make sure you understand the connections. Inspecting these terms in side-by-side columns adds clarity and hopefully will help those left behind in this regard quickly catch up.

View the next table, examine it carefully, then return to the discussion that follows.

Setting

"Where" gets reworded as "Location," "When" becomes "Time," and these two go together to form the "Setting" of the story.

Setting = Location + Time.

Characters

"Who" gets reworded as "Characters." The story still has a good guy and a bad one. The "Hero" becomes the "Protagonist," and the "Villain" becomes the "Antagonist." In addition, other characters get distinguished as either filing in to support the protagonist or standing on the side of the antagonists. Some characters may not neatly fit in these two categories of good and evil, so we will just group them as "Other."

Plot

"What" transforms into the "Plot" and takes on a more detailed verbiage to give depth to a storyline. In an exposition, the story gets introduced in a manner to promote interest without setting off any spoiler alerts.

As the plot or the "What" continues, the rising actions include the happenings of the story that climb in intensity. As the action increases in excitement, conflict enters the narrative within the rising action. Eventually, the protagonist triumphs (good over evil), creating a nice climax. Afterwards, the falling action can include things such as sharing about the victory or telling of winning to the other characters in the story. It can include cleaning up the street, locking up the antagonist along with the rest of the bad guys, and following up by coming to aid any characters that still need help.

The resolution, also part of the plot, conveys the outcome of the story and often includes acknowledgements such as a celebration, an awards ceremony, a triumphant phone call, or perhaps a simple cliff hanger. If a cliff hanger ends the story, then the narrative may not necessarily include a resolution. Stories with a cliffhanger at the end have increased in popularity for a series style of book writing. Cliffhangers, when done well, can whet the appetite of the readers so they anticipate the release of the next book in the series since the first had no solid closure.

Next, we will explore each of the main story parts and give you a chance to practice in your journal book even more. First, we will set out to strengthen the writing of the setting portion of the story.

Setting

Plan out the location and timing of the story with care. I imagine the location as a somewhat empty canvas upon which the writer starts crafting an artistic masterpiece. A sensory description of the environment around which the story begins unfolding will include purposefully selected adjectives. It could also include figurative language such as metaphors, similes, and personification.

Add the layer of time to the scene to help the reader imagine being there. Sunrise looks different than midnight. A sweaty hot summer trip up a mountain contrast greatly to a steep climb up a cold snowy covered boulder. As you begin building a setting, carefully weave location and time together. In the above example, I did not say the word January or winter, the scene description implied the season of the year. Writers can choose to spell out precisely the time and season or indicate it by using sensory descriptions. Does the setting change?

Yes, rarely will a book only have one setting. Characters move around to different places. The clock ticks, the timeline advances, so consider laying out story scenes. For each scene, develop a setting. New young writers must practice acquiring the patience for writing multiple scenes, each containing a new setting. Thus, one "where or location" might initially prove adequate. However, the appetite for more soon emerges for maturing writers. I invite you now to imagine having multiple scenes in a narrative story. Take time now to practice by coming up with more locations. These will serve as places for your narrative story to reside. You can add more places later. Also decide the time of season and time of day for visiting each of these places. Create separate journal entries to experiment with this concept. If feasible, you may even travel to locations if these exist in real life. Like the earlier exercises, challenge yourself to write in a sensory style. Enjoy the process! Include something in the journal entry to help you later recall the location.

Journal Entry – (Today's Date) — Under a Tree at Noon

Once you have finished practicing with one setting, go again. Create another one. When preparing to write a book, make sure to consider how to transition to the next setting. Do two bickering boys go outside to work out their differences? Does the mom walk a toddler up the stairs to prepare for bed? Perhaps a couple will go for a walk and end up in a nearby park. You decide. How will the characters end up in the next scene? Practice creating a new scene and include some sentences at the close of each to ease in this transition. You can decide on chapter titles for the scenes.

Journal Entry – (Today's Date)–12 am in the Basement

Characters may enter and others exit with each scene. Consider the role of entering and exiting characters. After completing the second setting or scene, transition to one that has either more characters or an entirely different set. Do not worry if this process feels a little bumpy. Keep practicing! In the next section, we will explore writing characters into the story. For now, just practice creating this new scene and spontaneously work with your characters.

Journal Entry – (Today's Date) –Fall Family Dining Rm

Now that you have an idea as to how to create the setting, continue experimenting. After completing the "setting" journal entries, you now have a better grasp of how to design the story's environment. Before proceeding, you may repeat the setting development journaling for each chapter scene or opt to come back to the remaining ones late. Next, we will focus attention on developing story characters.

Characters

Most stories contain several characters. Have you noticed how each character seems to have a different personality and a unique physical appearance? Designing and developing characters does take some time. However, with a little practice you can present your characters in such a way that the readers will feel well acquainted as if these people really exist. Start practicing by creating your own characters. Imagine which ones would most likely enter the settings you develop. Describe each character in detail. Weave these aspects together as the story unfolds. A fully descriptive narrative would include physical and personality attributes. It could also capture strengths and weaknesses, emotions, and thoughts. Additionally, consider including insights as to each character's way of life, family living, culture, national origin, beliefs, and anything else you feel helpful to the reader. Imagine introducing these people in person to the readers. Take time to capture your thoughts regarding potential characters for your story. For each journal entry, write about different characters.

Journal Entry – (Today's Date) – Character – Protagonist

Journal Entry – (Today's Date) – Character – Antagonist

Journal Entry – (Today's Date) – Character – Friend of Protagonist

---

Journal Entry – (Today's Date) – Character – Friend of Antagonist

---

Can you think of any other characters? Create additional journal entries for planning out the other characters.

Plot

Many beginning writers do express feelings of anxiety when writing a plot, especially if they do so for the first time. For our discussion, I will give you a basic start to build upon. Begin by engaging your imagination. You already have some starting setting descriptions. You have ideas for the characters. Now imagine a movie playing. These characters will now interact in the environment you have designed. What can you imagine them doing? Who likes each other? Who does not get along? What types of weaknesses should the readers see, especially in the

28

antagonist? What types of strengths should they see, especially in the protagonist? Picture your characters moving around from location to location, or scene to scene. Where do they begin? What crazy thing happens? Each scene or location can end up being a chapter in a book. Consider the following table as you plan:

Chapter	Setting	Characters	What happens here?	Strengths/Weaknesses, conflicts
(Add a row for each chapter.)				

Complete the table allowing your mind space for capturing your thoughts. The strengths, weaknesses, and conflict columns should keep readers on the edge of the chair. This happened, then this happened. Next, can you believe it, this happened. You get the idea. The action should rise or increase along the way. You will need a victory chapter in which the protagonist wins the challenge. Afterwards, include a chapter for falling action: cleaning up messes, locking up the bad guys, and letting everyone know things look normal. Reserve the final resolution chapter for a celebration of sorts. Go ahead and practice by creating a planning table in your journal book. Just do your best and have fun in the process!

Journal Entry – (Today's Date) – Plot – Plot Planning Table

Theme and Morals

While writer perspectives do differ in beliefs regarding themes and morals, I think of themes more like filing folder type of categories. If your story contains scenes in which the characters learn that cheating on a test will earn them bad grades and that lying will get them suspended from school, you may decide to pick "honesty" as the theme.

The morals in this case would include the two lessons: Do not cheat and tell the truth. Your narrative story can contain many lessons. These lessons we call morals. As you group the lessons into categories, we will call these groups the themes of the story. You can imagine these lessons or morals fitting inside of each of your imaginary theme labeled folders.

Take some time to practice. First, it might prove helpful to consider the target age of your readers. Will people your own age or younger read your book? Consider that age group or that type of reading audience. What could help them in life? If you do get stuck, I recommend browsing the internet. You can search for articles and reports on "lessons for teens," "lessons for young adults," "lessons for kids," and so forth. Pick some of these, then as you develop the characters, purposefully plan for one or more characters to have weaknesses. Additionally, develop empathy. Listen to happenings in your circle of influence, in your community. Pay attention to trials and victories experienced by real people. Improve your plot by writing about events that occur in which these types of problems arise. Of course, change the details and the names.

Overall, the book you write becomes the stage upon which you share your convictions. Your characters act out the roles and life experiences you, the author, design.

Also, how could the characters mature and learn not to make the same mistakes again? As the saying goes, no one is perfect. However, we do not want to repeatedly make the same mistakes. By the end of the book, the readers should have a sense of the lessons to learn and hopefully connect and feel for those in the story, especially the ones that successfully did learn these lessons.

Take some time now to practice and work with building ideas for themes and morals. Search the internet or use your own experience to do some planning. Complete the following journal entries as you practice. For this next journal entry, make a list of all the life trials, victories, and lessons you would like to possibly include in your story.

Journal Entry – (Today's Date) – Morals – Life Lessons to Share

---

For the next journal entry, consider which life lessons could go together in a group. These groups you will put a title on, such as honesty, kindness, and perseverance. Make a list of your themes and match them to the morals or lessons.

Journal Entry – (Today's Date) – Theme – My Lesson Groups

Next, can you already begin to imagine which characters will learn these lessons in your story? Can you think of the settings that each of these lessons appear in for the readers to notice? If so, make some notes about chapter numbers or settings and characters in this next journal entry. For some writers, this step comes later during their writing process. So, do not feel pressured to decide all this right now.

You now have plans for a nice narrative. Enjoy drafting out each chapter and follow the plans that you have placed in the journal entries. Again, writing narrative stories does take a little practice, so please enjoy the process, and write, write, and write some more.

Summary

By progressing from the basic 5Ws to the use of upper-level writing, students often set out to create longer written pieces such as those found in narrative books. In this chapter, you have experimented with planning out the setting, characters, plot, theme, and morals for a narrative story. Be encouraged to turn these plans into a book and creatively make use of your imagination. Writing does take practice, so enjoy the adventure, write often, and remain persistent. One thing shines for you while continuing to write, that one thing has to do with identity. Writing helps us discover more about ourselves. Such a discovery warrants an entire section in this book. Journey forward to the next section.

Chapter Questions

1. List each of the 5Ws. Next to each one, write the new wording used by more advanced writers.

2. You have been asked to write a story that takes place in a lovely garden during the springtime. How would you describe the setting? Write your answer in sentence form.

3. Look at the sentences you just wrote for the setting. Circle or underline descriptive words that help the reader mentally see the lovely setting. What other words can you add to further help the reader enjoy this environment?

4. Define the following terms:

   protagonist

   antagonist

5. Imagine an antagonist messing up your beautiful garden. Help the reader get acquainted with the antagonist, then write the dreadful scene in which the garden becomes damaged.

6. Thankfully, the protagonist comes to rescue in time to save the garden. Identify good character qualities in the protagonist and write the rescue scene.

7. Write a compelling ending for your story, making sure to include a nice moral and a celebration. Explain your story's moral and theme.

As you develop writing skills, make it a personal goal to add an interesting flow to your paragraphs by applying different sentence structures.

Chapter 4 Sentence Structure

Chapter Objectives

- Demonstrate necessary skills for writing simple, compound, and complex sentences.

- Identify the requirements for creating three types of sentences: simple, compound, and complex.

- Distinguish between a dependent and independent clause.

- Explore how to use coordinating and subordinate conjunctions.

- Discuss the rationale behind varying sentence structures.

Have you noticed the rhythm of sentences? Many of us, including me, unknowingly write favoring a particular sentence structure. Challenge yourself to add variety by switching things up. Write using simple, compound, and complex sentences. Alternate the ordering! After all, a paragraph full of only simple sentences could sound boring to the reader. Take some time to review these three common sentence structures.

Simple Sentence

A simple sentence contains one complete thought, also known as an independent clause.

Beautiful yellow sunflowers grow wildly.

Imagine five different story scenes taking place in various locations. Write one simple sentence to go with each scene for a total of five sentences. You will add more sentences soon!

Journal Entry – (Today's Date) – Simple Sentence Practice

Compound Sentence

Write two complete thoughts, then join these together using a comma and a coordinating conjunction.

Beautiful yellow sunflowers grow wildly. (simple = one thought)

Melodious sparrows chirp, and chattering squirrels store acorns. (compound = two thoughts)

Review this list of common coordinating conjunctions:

- for
- and
- nor
- but
- or
- yet
- so

NOTE: Think of FANBOYS to help you remember.

Test in out. Refer to the last journal entry and the five scenes. Can you add a compound sentence to each scene?

You should have at least ten sentences, two for each scene. You have five scenes, and each of these has a simple sentence and a compound sentence. Next, examine how to create a complex sentence.

Complex Sentence

A complex sentence consists of one dependent and one independent clause. It contains one incomplete thought and another complete thought. If the dependent, the incomplete thought goes first, remember to include a comma.

Beautiful yellow sunflowers grow wildly. (simple sentence = one thought)

Melodious sparrows chirp, and chattering squirrels store acorns. (compound sentence = two thoughts)

Although her surroundings appear peaceful, Judy Lynn Brooks sits weeping. (complex sentence = one incomplete thought and a complete one)

Do you see the word "although?" The dependent clause begins with this subordinate conjunction. The English language has many subordinate conjunctions. The common ones will help you get started. Take time to review the subordinate conjunctions before continuing.

- If
- Since
- As
- When
- Although
- While
- After
- Before
- Until
- Because

Look at this sentence written in two ways.

Although her surroundings appear peaceful, Judy Lynn Brooks sits weeping. **(complex sentence with the dependent clause first)**

Judy Lynn Brooks sits weeping although her surroundings appear peaceful. **(complex sentence with the dependent clause last)**

Most writers agree that if the dependent clause gets placed at the end, then take away the comma. The exception to the rule has to do with writing using interrupters or additional phrases. You may practice writing complex sentences both ways.

Recall the five scenes developed over the last two journal entries. Practice adding a complex sentence to each scene. You can switch the order up to add an even nicer variety.

Journal Entry – (Today's Date) – Complex Sentence Practice

By the end of your practice, you should have at least fifteen sentences, three for each scene. You should end up with at least five of each type of sentence: simple, compound, and complex.

Summary

As you develop writing skills, make it a personal goal to add an interesting flow to your paragraphs by applying different sentence structures. Include simple sentences. Introduce compound sentences that contain two independent clauses, and you can create a variance by adding other sentences that we would classify as complex. Continuing to practice writing and following the suggestions presented will enable you to develop excellent skills. Proceed to the next section to explore how to have a great sense of identity and tips on presenting yourself well.

Chapter Questions

1. List three types of sentence structure explained in this chapter.

2. Write about one of your most interesting days. Be sure to vary the overall structure by including a mixture of simple, compound, and complex sentences.

3. Define simple sentence and give an example.

4. Define compound sentence and give an example.

5. Explain the meaning of a complex sentence and give an example.

6. What is a coordinating conjunction and when would you use it?

7. Which type of sentence includes a subordinate conjunction? Give an example.

8. Make a list of coordinating conjunctions.

9. Make a list of subordinate conjunctions.

Section 2: Your Identity

I am sure the question of identity has already arisen in your lifetime. People stop and ask, some genuinely desire to get to know you, others just chit-chatting to pass the time or to come across as polite. In any case, having a better sense of yourself and possessing the ability to communicate such an introduction well, will help to shape future opportunities. In addition, the preparation involved, as laid out ahead, should provide solid grounds for purposefully moving forward in life. I have carefully thought out how to present the material in a manner that will help you find your sweet spot, learn more about yourself, and begin taking steps to properly share with others. Enjoy!

. You, yes, you play the starring role. Welcome to the beautiful discovery process and the writing of your story!

Chapter 5 Your Personal Discovery

Chapter Objectives

- Discover your sweet spot. Explain the meaning of sweet spot.

- Complete a self-discovery inventory.

- Recognize patterns in life that give clues as to your sweet spot.

An exploration journey would not possibly be complete without searching deep within and discovering more about oneself. By the end of this chapter, some of the same skills utilized earlier will now impact on nonfiction writing. You, yes, you play the starring role. Welcome to the beautiful discovery process and the writing of your story!

Over the years, I have personally enjoyed getting to know many individuals: students, professionals, and just regular folk. The discovery process we will now undertake has repeatedly been proven valuable by people in my circle of influence. Many have expressed so much appreciation and have shared with me that these exercises have tremendously helped in paving the way for the future. I count it an honor and a joy to now invite you on a personal discovery of yourself.

What do you love to do or think you would enjoy doing?

Again, open your journal book, and write your responses to the questions, "What do I love doing? What would I love to do?" Please do not hold back. Include everything imaginable. Where would you like to travel? What hobbies do you enjoy? Would you like to go see some plays or musicals? Would you like to attend a particular school or take a class? Do you enjoy learning new strategies? Have you considered speaking a different language? Do you experiment with cooking? Maybe sports are your thing? Do you love talking with people? Are you an investigator at heart? Do you enjoy reading or writing? What kinds of work or career positions might look appealing? Keep going... Do you imagine yourself getting married and having kids? This is your time to really, really dream! Dream big! Think long! Write it all down. GO!

Journal Entry – (Today's Date) - What do I love?

Did anything surprise you? Did anything stand out as huge, maybe something that you absolutely must take time to do? Please make sure to fully complete the prior journal entry before proceeding to the next one.

(No Spoilers – Don't look ahead!)

The first question involved exploring what floats your boat, what makes life enjoyable for you. Now, take the next step. What skills do you possess? How did you gain each of these skills? So, for this section you may list things like, "Playing piano." If playing piano is one of your skills, please make sure to also include some extra details. How long have you been playing piano? How did you acquire such an education? Did you take a particular class? Did you attend private lessons? Are you self-taught? In this next section, make an inventory of all your talents and skills. Include an explanation of the level of experience and where you received the training. Additionally, please add to the list anything you would like to develop and would be willing to take a class or receive further education or training to develop the skills. Are you ready for your skills inventory journal entry? Please proceed. Again, make sure not to hold back. Yes, that cooking class that you took two summers ago does count! That honors English 101 class counts too! Your digital arts summer class goes here as well!

Journal Entry – (Today's Date) – What do I know?

Did you finish? How much information did you write? If you do not have very much, please continue this discovery exercise after taking a break. When individuals do not write much in response to these discovery questions, I have noticed it often has to do with the state of the person. Tiredness, weariness, hunger, etc., all of these can impede responses. Try your best to include all your skills and expertise. Please make sure to fully complete the prior journal entry before proceeding to the next one. Do you know how to speak more than one language? Perhaps baking desserts, mowing lawns, writing gaming programs, or scoring high on algebra might make the list.

(No Spoilers – Don't look ahead!)

Congratulations! The first two journal entries for this chapter may have felt taxing and required pouring out your soul onto the page. However, I am sure you agree with me. This date stamped journal entry meaningfully signifies a level of maturity that may be new to you.

As your current mentor, I have one more question to ask you. After you carefully answer it, then we can begin to put some pieces together. Shall we continue to answer the next question?

What needs do you see in your circle of influence, your family's business, and in the surrounding community?

Take time to explore the world around you. For this discovery section, feel free to interview people, browse the internet, check out news articles, media, books, and more. Consider this a safari hunt. We live in a time in which some solutions rank higher than others. Some intelligent resources become scarce and needed by multiple people at the same time. In case you have not figured it out yet, I am speaking about professions, careers, about fields of study. I am speaking about gaps in our own communities, schools, governments, businesses, and in society around us. As you look around, do you see interesting needs that perhaps would make sense for you to step in and solve? What types of workers does your own neighborhood need right now? What types of job postings appear noting current openings? What types of careers rise above the rest because of the high demand for staffing? Before answering, please do some research. Browse and check things out and add details to your next journal entry. Please do this next part very carefully and with intentionality. Enjoy the journey! If you plan to work in a family business or own your own, still complete this exploration. After all, such an organization will want to meet the needs of its clients – the community.

Journal Entry – (Today's Date) – What's in demand?

Please make sure to fully complete the prior journal entry before proceeding to the next one.

(No Spoilers – Don't look ahead!)

Find the common ground – Your sweet spot!

Thank you for responding to the three in-depth discovery questions.

Now, look through your journal entries for this personal discovery.

Notice trends! Did anything appear uniformly across all three journal

entries? For example, if "Chemistry" showed up on each of these three

journal entries, then that stands out as a very important consideration.

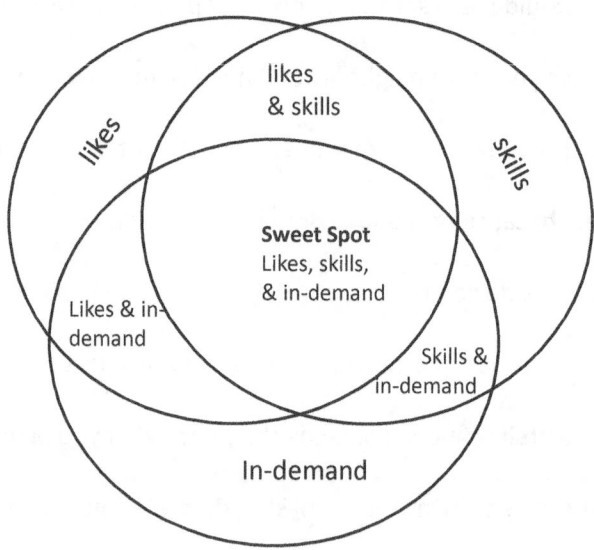

Go through and highlight, put stars around it, or simply make special notes of any recurring points, mentions, passions, or interests found in your journal. You may even want to create a Venn diagram. If so, draw three large overlapping circles on a page in your journal, and label them: my likes, my skills, and in-demand. The likes circle should overlap with the skills circle and the in-demand circles.

I recommend that you browse the internet to review a variety of Venn diagrams. The things that end up in all three journals (likes, skills, and in-demand), will appear in the middle of the Venn diagram. These we will refer to as your **sweet spot**. Summarize your highest interests, desires, and most importantly, future goals shaped by in-demand needs.

Many people have gone through these discovery questions with me, most have all similarly ended by having concrete starting points for either beginning or advancing their course of study or career. Record these summary thoughts in the next journal entry. These will serve as goals for the future. Additionally, you will make use of the indicated sweet spot in creating a portfolio.

Journal Entry – (Today's Date) – Sweet Spot

Now, with goals in hand, journey on and explore how to create a portfolio that will represent your overall makeup, your skills, talents, and abilities. Armed with a unique desire, your sweet spot-- that which inspires, motivates, and propels you towards the future – now focus on career development in a way that best takes these aspects into consideration.

Did you enjoy discovering your sweet spot? In working with many people over the years, repeatedly, this exercise has proved valuable. In my own journey, I first learned about this concept from reading Jim Collins' book entitled, Good to Great.[1] Jim Collins' teaches his leadership principle, "The Hedgehog Concept" in a similar manner to how I now present the sweet spot. Clearly, identifying your sweet spot and communicating it well to others should help wisely advance your career.

Summary

In this chapter, you took a self-discovery inventory of what you love, of your skill sets, and assessed the in-demand needs of the world around you. The overlapping items gave an indication of your potential

---

[1] (Collins 2001)

sweet spot. In the upcoming chapters, gain skills in presenting yourself to others. You will want to communicate your sweet spot in different settings.

Chapter Questions

1. Explain the meaning of the term sweet spot.

2. Describe how self-inventory helps in discovering your sweet spot.

3. Did anything surprise you about your answers to the self-discovery questions?

4. Can knowing your sweet spot help you in moving forward? Explain.

By the end of the book, hopefully your portfolio will paint a picture of you! It will capture passions, desires, ambitions, skills, abilities, dreams, hopes, and career aspirations. Enjoy the building process!

Chapter 6 Portfolio Creation and Showcase

Chapter Objectives

- Explore available portfolio building sites and study the associated tutorials.

- Create a category list for best representing yourself in the portfolio.

- Within each category, identify page contents to showcase.

- Define portfolio and explain reasons for having one.

I really had no clue as to what a portfolio entails until embarking on a quest to earn my master's degree. Tip toeing into this chapter, my thoughts race back to folders of neatly ordered papers and materials. Such papers often consisted of a carefully crafted resume, letters of introduction, references from leaders, samples of my work, and a sheet filled with contact information of people who would speak favorably of me should special phone or in person interviews occur.

Thankfully, much of this kind of information tracking now takes place online! Whew, I cannot begin to share in-depth how much this newer way of doing things will make your life so much easier! The caveat lies in taking time to properly gather inputs and beautifully organize them to showcase your work. You will want to share or present your dreams and your passions in a meaningful manner. Ready to dream? Proceed forward!

Your Portfolio

Given the latest technological advancements, creating a portfolio provides a convenient way to package your expertise together and introduce yourself to future employers, prospective universities, academic award types of competitions, potential clients, and to any progressive establishment. In the last chapter, you discovered and solidified the overall things that uniquely define your makeup. Keeping this in the forefront of thought, design a digital menu of sorts to host contributions and examples of your work, a resume, references from people that know you, your hobbies, academic and business-related projects, volunteer efforts, community services, awards, and trophies, etc. Take time now to look back at each of the main highlights made during your personal discovery process. Carefully consider what you wrote on the journal pages.

Main Categories

Look at what you wrote to describe your "sweet spot." Can you now make category names for each main thing you listed as a "like" or "skill" that matches your "goals" and sits in the center spot?" For example, you may be interested in writing books, pursuing a business degree, and performing on the side using your piano skills. Categories could therefore be something like Writing Books, Future in Business, and Piano Performance. Students can include sections on Academic Projects and Presentations. Take some time to make a note of each category in a new journal entry. You may find it helpful to also write down reminders of why you selected such a category.

Each of the categories represents a page or group of pages in your portfolio. Imagine each category like a digital file folder. The items in your portfolio can be sorted into these.

Journal Entry – (Today's Date) - Gathering Inputs for the Portfolio

---

Take a moment to decide on your categories before continuing in this lesson.

Category	School Projects	Community Service	Piano
Pieces (pages)	- Writings - Computer Programs - Science Fairs	- Kids camp helper - Toy drive - Walkathon	- Recital - Awards - Created songs

Gathering Pieces

Now, with your new categories in hand, think back to all the things you have done so far in life. You will want to find things to put into each category. These things can include school activities and class projects, community participation kinds of activities, and your own personal hobby involvement. Especially consider anything that would match up, or fit underneath any of your new categories. Do you have any artwork, essays, science projects, community service awards, etc.? List these in the journal as well. Do not limit yourself to only paper types of items. Remember, music recital materials, acting scripts, etc. can end up in a video clip or podcast kind of media. Your list can and should include different kinds of media. Take your ideas and match them to the categories. These entries become inputs for the portfolio. Include thoughts as to what accomplishments or classes of study, etcetera could land in each category. What would you like to showcase?

After exhausting all thoughts and ideas for what to gather or the performances from the past moments of life to include, ask yourself what you could create or plan out for adding to the portfolio in the future---hopefully the near future. Add these entries to your journal list and match them to the appropriate categories.

Building the Portfolio

While writing this book, several options exist for building and presenting portfolios online. Find your favorite by searching the internet for "portfolios and websites free." If you are reading this book as part of a class requirement, ask your teacher or professor for recommendations. Building a portfolio does take some skills to get started. Most of the portfolio building tools come with getting started instructions. The categories you listed earlier serve as nice clickable menu items that visitors to the portfolio can click on to open. When the visitor clicks on a menu item, behind the click sits a URL link, this connects to your actual online page that holds the work for display.

For example, your portfolio may have links or tabs labeled *School Projects, The Arts, Community Service, My Published Books.*

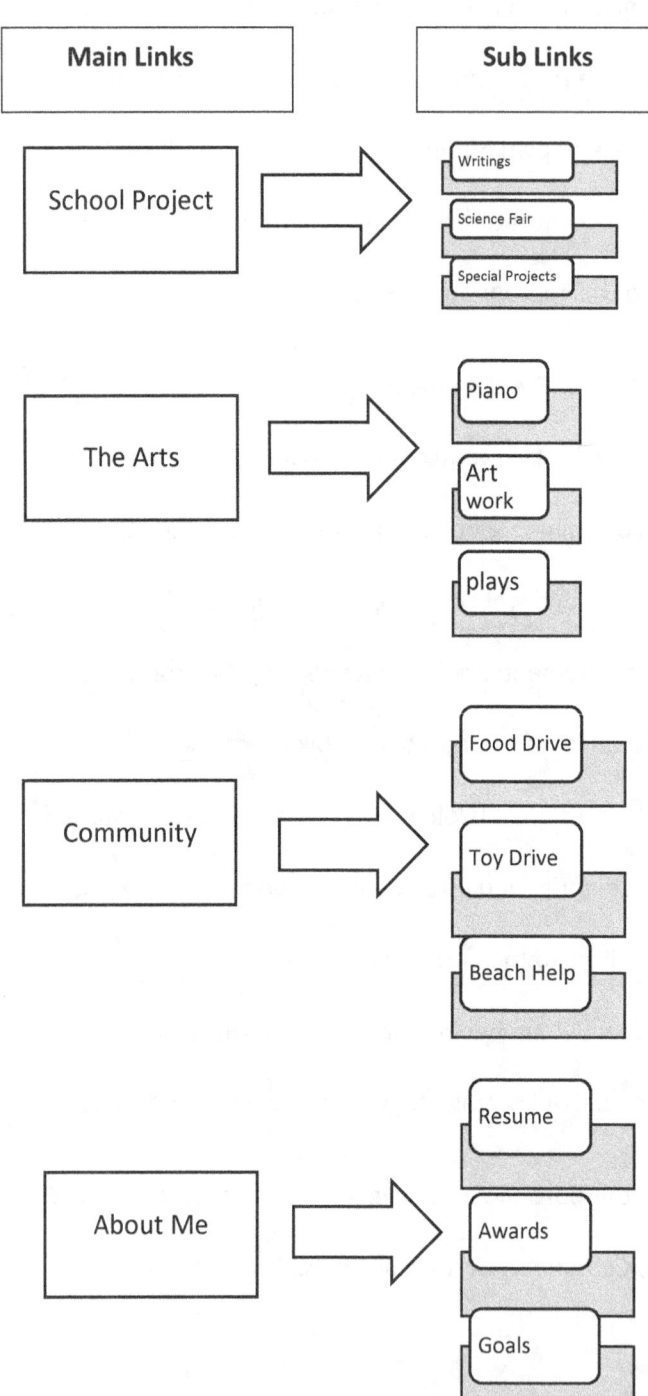

Main Links	Sub Links
School Project	Writings
	Science Fair
	Special Projects
The Arts	Piano
	Art work
	plays
Community	Food Drive
	Toy Drive
	Beach Help
About Me	Resume
	Awards
	Goals

Once clicked, each could take the visitor to the next level on which you can have links to pages. The pages would each contain a sample of your work and more.

The page may contain a video clip of your favorite violin solo. A page may contain an essay that received favorable marks. Perhaps, a picture of a community service award along with a written explanation of how you received it might appear on another page. Each of these pages get accessed from a menu. The menu holds the links to the pages.

After listing out your categories (perspective menu clicks), and portfolio input candidates (your essays, projects, artwork, etc.) take time to learn about the portfolio building tools currently available. Search the internet, find the "Getting started" tutorial, and begin that part of your journey.

Populating the Portfolio

After deciding what to include in the portfolio, begin uploading content one category at a time. Again, you will want to refer to the tutorials provided by the vendor and others that best illustrate and explain how to load the content.

Summary

We will plan to revisit the topic of the portfolio at the end of the book. By presenting the portfolio idea early in the book, the reader will hopefully take time to start gathering all the items noted earlier and begin building one. You will want to keep building consistently. Add more content along the way. We will return to the presentation component in the concluding section of the book. By the end of the book, hopefully your portfolio will paint a picture of you! It will capture passions, desires, ambitions, skills, abilities, dreams, hopes, and career aspirations. Enjoy the building process! Continue!

Chapter Questions

1. Define portfolio.

2. Why should you build a portfolio?

3. Map out your portfolio. Begin with a list of categories. Explain why you have chosen each category.

4. For each category, what do you wish to include? Make a list of content pages.

5. Why would it be helpful to continue adding content periodically to the portfolio?

6. What types of media can go on a portfolio page?

Section 3: Listen and Take Notes

Has anyone ever sat down and taught you how to listen? Now, before you begin to laugh, think about it. We live in a society in which most of us find ourselves rushing here and there, hardly with time to really listen well. Sounds blur into each other in a cacophony of confusion of sorts. No wonder many individuals feel ignored, neglected, or not heard. The need for listening well has increased in our rushed environment. Another problem remaining has to do with remembering it all. Listening well does not always mean you will remember the information. In this section, we will explore the art of listening and note taking. The information received becomes valuable as you organize it for retention and for later use. Stop all the distractions for a while, and travel on. Let me share with you some thoughts about listening well and remembering.

Every day, our minds must decipher

and act as traffic controllers,

directing, navigating, and

prioritizing attention to the variety

of inputs in our environment.

Chapter 7 Attentiveness

Chapter Objectives

- Identify the benefits of listening effectively.

- Describe the roadblocks standing in the way of careful listening.

- Explore tips for developing higher levels of listening.

- Practice, practice, and practice again. Practice listening and taking notes. By doing so, you increase your competency in this area.

- Explain the connection between careful listening and improved relationships.

The beginning chapters of this book encouraged the development of sensory writing skills. Carefully tuning into every sense helped you creatively come up with all kinds of things to include in your journal. I am sure you will agree that to the degree our ears listen, our eyes see, and our fingers feel, we can descriptively write an account of events, places, things, and even include our own thoughts and feelings in such creative expression. We can take our observations and internalize them.

Hearing and seeing do not take place only outside of the physical body. Self-talk, the inward chattering, continues to play out daily. Mental images, like tiny movie scenes run constantly. Every day, our minds must decipher and act as traffic controllers, directing, navigating, and prioritizing attention to the variety of inputs in our environment.

Daydreaming, Distracted, and Tuned Out

In the classroom, or perhaps in a business location, or even at a family discussion around the dinner table, listeners face the challenge of tuning in to the appropriate messages. Not fully paying attention could occur because of processing and "listening to" internal thoughts that inwardly sound louder than the voice of the actual speaker.

For example, if a mother calls out, "Hey, Susan, did you even hear a word I just said?" -- more than likely, the mother did speak in an audible voice. However, the teen got distracted by her own personal mental thoughts.

Inside a classroom, listening to a lecture, students find themselves drifting away even further. Did the student even notice the visual diagram presented by the teacher? No, despite a desire to absorb the lesson, an unfocused brain entertains mental movie clips of the best place to eat lunch, the next movie to watch, or perhaps a cool hiking location to check out alongside a distant mountain. If the student desires to earn good grades, these self-propelled inward movie clips must mentally stream only at proper times.

In the prior chapters, you discovered unique attributes of your own future desires. Seeing these come to fruition will require developing a focused mind. Undoubtedly, within the list of dreams and goals, weaving into your future tapestry, the need to attend lectures or classroom presentations has materialized. Many career minded individuals discover that intermingled amongst the thrilling, exciting, and "can't wait!" types of classes, some courses or required subjects may offer a degree of "boring" challenges. We all encounter circumstances that require us to pay attention, intently focus, and listen to either boring speakers or perhaps someone talking at such an advanced level that we feel clueless. Additionally, often people come to lecture classes really interested in the subject, but lack the skills required for absorbing all that the dedicated professionals dishes out during the sessions. So, how can you strengthen personal attentiveness? Consider the following tips:

Attentiveness Tips

✓ Pay attention to the speaker even if the person speaks slowly or extremely fast.

67

- ✓ Put mental cloud hopping in check by taking notes of the presentation.
- ✓ Allow yourself an ample opportunity to indulge in personal daydreaming at a more appropriate time.
- ✓ Consider recording the presentation and listen again to pick up on key points.

Try It!

Practice, practice, and practice! Search through the internet or your favorite listening media, and select presentations of various lengths to watch, listen to, and take notes. At the time of this writing, one might find some good selections on the TED Talks website.[2] You can browse the internet for these talks or find something similar. Take notes to the extent that if given a quiz on the presentation, you would ace it in style! Or, even better, considering what you have heard, could you stand up and share important observations, considerations, thoughts, perspectives, and insights? Write verbatim any quotes that might prove

---

[2] (TED Conference, LLC n.d.)

citation worthy in a future essay assignment. This will require pausing the audio and backtracking, rewinding, to relisten to sections.

If possible, do this exercise with a group of people, and pair up afterwards to compare notes. Did you hear and see the same things? Did anything surprise you about note taking? Take time to discuss any new insights. Record your thoughts as a new journal entry.

Journal Entry – (Today's Date) – (Title of practice presentation)

Think about it.

Does listening attentively provide any benefits to you, to your friends and family, and to the community? As we wrap up this segment on listening, take time to record your thoughts. Did you learn anything new about listening worth taking with you into the future?

Journal Entry – (Today's Date) – Benefits of Careful Listening

---

To further strengthen your listening skills, listen to more presentations and practice note taking. If you decided to listen to the TED Talks, then challenge yourself to pick at least one "talk" from each major category: technology, entertainment, design, business, and global issues. Pay careful attention to which subjects present the most challenges in terms of note taking and paying attention. You will want to practice these areas more.

In Person Listening

Careful listening does require a higher level of attentiveness. When meeting individuals one-on-one, intense listening also communicates a sense of respect and care for the other person. Friendships and relationships excel when each feels the other effectively listens. Much like planting seeds in the soil, developing listening skills early in life will yield a growing future.

Relationships and Listening

Can you think of a time when listening carefully made a difference? Stephen Covey's book entitled Seven Habits of Highly Effective People helped me develop a more empathetic ear when interacting with other people (2020). "Seek first to understand before being understood." Mr. Covey explained that we often begin mentally rehearsing verbal responses or even jump in and interrupt before the other person has finished speaking. Effective listening requires that we first wait and listen to the other person and let her finish before formulating a response. Ideally, we should listen carefully, seek clarification, and show respect before inserting our own perspective. I attest to this exercise, though important, it presents a challenge for me. I must continually work on improving communications. Listening well means communicating well.

Certainly, listening also proves valuable when taking notes. Note taking has its own set of challenges. Travel on to the next chapter to discover some helpful strategies. You will want to practice taking notes again after completing the next two chapters.

Summary

Listening, when done intently, effectively helps to advance relationships, improve understanding of materials, enhances note taking, communicates respect, and shows an increased level of maturity. Listening takes patience, practice, and a willingness to hear the thoughts of those you come in contact in your circle of everyday life. It also opens the door to greater opportunities in your future. Organizations, leaders, future oriented education programs all look forward to welcoming people to join them that care enough to really listen! As mentioned, listening helps to improve note taking skills. In the next chapter, we will explore some tips for further excelling your note taking abilities.

Chapter Questions

1. List some of the benefits of effective listening. Underline the ones that apply to you the most.

2. Explain at least two ways to improve your listening skills.

3. This chapter mentioned the Ted Talks site as a resource to access for practicing listening. Make a list of audios or videos you would like to use to personally practice listening. Set time aside on your schedule to carry out such practice.

4. Think through conversations you have been a part of recently. Explain the importance of listening on at least one of these occasions.

5. How could better listening help you in maturing as a person or developing one or more-character traits?

Personally, mapping thoughts and project ideas really inspires me to squeeze the sponge and think creatively.

Chapter 8 Note Taking

Chapter Objectives

- Create your own personal shorthand system for use in note taking and explain why using it increases efficiency.

- Share why you think the Cornell Method has grown in popularity and design your own note taking template.

- Demonstrate the use of thought mapping. Show how incorporating this method can enhance note taking.

- Explain the benefit of combining a personal shorthand system, use of a note taking template, and thought mapping or visual representation.

- Explain how using an outline method can prove helpful, especially for longer notes or report preparations.

While listening to lectures, presentations, and other types of discussions, take notes. Some popular note taking strategies to consider follow:

- ✓ Create a personal shorthand system.
- ✓ Cornell Method
- ✓ Thought mapping
- ✓ Sketching/Diagraming
- ✓ Outlining

In your last journal entry, you took notes. Did you incorporate any special method for taking these notes? In this chapter, we will explore ways to fine-tune your note taking skills. Educators and scholars have written much on these strategies. You may have even already used one or more of these. We will review each briefly. While professionals debate as to which to call the best, it really comes down to how you personally learn. If you prefer a visual approach to learning new materials, then thought mapping, sketching, or diagramming might prove most effective. On the other hand, if you tend to skip past drawings and go straight to reading text, then the Cornell Method or outlining may work better. Though each person may have a preference between visual pictorial or logical details, both approaches when combined create more of a wholistic perspective. Take time to review these note-taking tips and test them out for yourself.

Create a personal shorthand system.

Professors in colleges and universities often spend hours preparing for one hour of lecture time. In other words, those three chapters you just finished reading as part of last week's assignment, now get presented in class in an hour. Obviously, the professor will not read the three chapters out loud to you. The lecture will most likely include the main ideas, important details associated with this reading, and extra thoughts contributed by the professor through personal experience. If the speaker, the professor in this case, talks quickly, students may feel tempted not to write any notes at all.

They reason, "I can read chapters 1 through 3 after class," or "I already read the first three chapters before this class."

This rationale does have pitfalls. First, taking notes in class allows the student to capture which aspects the professor considers important. These critical thoughts become candidates for testing material. Secondly, taking notes will ensure the inclusion of new materials provided by the professor that the book did not cover.

Instead of choosing not to take notes, the recommended approach includes creating your own system to aid in writing more quickly. For example, a lower-case w, when written by itself, might stand for the word "with." A lower-case t, might stand for "together."

Creating your own shorthand system works nicely if the abbreviated versions of words chosen get recorded in a dictionary kind of look up cheat-sheet.

Note Taking Personal Shorthand Example			
w/	with	.:	therefore
fr	from	* (use	test candidate
w/o	without	color)	item in list
w/i	within	-	
def	definition	ASAP	as soon as possible
ex	example	b/c	because
ie	that is	vs	versus/contrast
re	regarding		
etc	and so on	btwn	between
yr	year	qty	quantity
p/pp	page/ pages	N	number of people
imp	important	min	minimum/ minutes
ref	reference	max	maximum
reg	regular	#	number
prob	problem	X	times
>	greater	↓	decrease/ down
<	less	↑	increase/ up
->	leads to	=	like, alike, equals
		Ea	each
		incl	include

Otherwise, when studying for the final exam, you may forget what your abbreviations mean. Alternatively, you may browse the internet in search of "shorthand for note taking." Upon searching, do you see the different ideas? Pick the symbols and shorthand abbreviations that work best for you. Make up your own. Having this available during note-taking sessions could speed up the writing process.

Take the plunge, the challenge! Select another Ted Talk or something similar, listen to it, and use your new shorthand system to aid you in taking notes. It does take practice! At first, you may find yourself proceeding slowly. Keep practicing! Allow yourself time to grow accustomed to the new system.

Journal Entry – (Today's Date) – My Shorthand Practice

Many of the note taking techniques overlap, meaning you can combine them. Liven up the formatting of your note taking paper and continue with the shorthand system by incorporating the Cornell Method.

Cornell Method

Have you tried the famous Cornell Method?[3] Browsing the internet for this approach will unveil descriptions and even various preprinted paper options. Some vendors even promote computer templates for you to use digitally. So, how did this method originate?

Professor Walter Pauk, from the University of Cornell, developed it as a flexible way for students to capture notes. Currently the University of Cornell's website does contain free videos and short classes on the effective use of this note taking method. Browsing the internet, one can

---

[3] (Cornell University n.d.)

see different variations for the page layout. Overall, the three common sections include a smaller left "Cue" section, a larger right "Note" section, and a bottom or page footer "Summary" section. Take time to browse the internet for Cornell note taking to see some visual images.

The "Note" section contains written thoughts, diagrams, and ideas captured from listening to a lecture or even from reading materials such as a chapter in a textbook. The "Cue" section on the left contains brief reminders such as a question to ask, vocabulary words to understand, or other important reminders. The "Cue" section serves as a quick way of reviewing the notes written as a whole. The "Summary" section captures the main overall ideas. Do you have a textbook chapter assigned, perhaps from one of your current classes? As you read, practice this new Cornell method.

Over time, many have customized the note taking page to their own liking. For example, you may desire to have a doodling, mapping, sketching section set aside on your paper. I would highly recommend adding the date, day, and perhaps the course number to the top right corner of the header and placing the title either to the top left or middle.

Title	Date/Day/Class
Key Points	Main Ideas and Details

Doodle, map, sketch

Summary

Take a moment to design your own template. Sketch it out in your journal now. You may even decide to creatively design a template for easy printing.

Journal Entry – (Today's Date) – My Note Taking Template

Some of the modifications to the Cornell note taking might arise due to the need to express thought graphically or pictorially. Continue building on your note taking skills by developing your own toolkit. Keep using your personal shorthand system, enjoy having your note taking template, now add in a visual perspective by including some thought maps.

Thought Maps

Thought mapping, aka mind mapping, offers the flexibility of allowing for a visual display of connection between ideas, thoughts, steps, sequences, and progressions. At the time of this writing, this author's personal favorite mind mapping software, Mind Manager, costs quite a penny.[4] The essential edition subscription has a $99 a year price tag on it, while the professional one goes for $169 annually. It offers the flexibility of expanding and collapsing the branches of the map. Its "presentation mode" also provides a convenient way to step attendees through flowing content during a meeting. The export features allow for taking the branches or thoughts and bringing them into project

---

[4] (Corel Corporation n.d.)

management software, slide presentations, Word documents, and more. Other thought mapping tools exist today. Take time to browse the internet and explore these. Several companies offer free versions of their products with hopes of enticing you to purchase the more complete edition. Still, paper and pencil prove adequate means for most students desiring to capture notes, thoughts, ideas, and more. Maps can grow and grow and grow and grow and grow! Some tools to consider when embarking on manually creating thought maps on paper follow:

✓ large blank sheets of paper or a large desk size pad of paper

✓ colorful pens, pencils, highlighters, markers

✓ ruler, shape object stencils

✓ large open space on a table or desk

Browse the internet for "thought mapping images," and see a wide variety of styles. You can quickly learn the classic approach.

✓ Simply write a title for your topic in the middle of a huge sheet of paper, and draw a circle, oval, or other desired shape around your writing.

✓ Next, mentally divide this main topic into its subcomponents or parts. Give each of these a name. These part names become the branches that sit around the main core title. For example, if assessing communication strategies, you might have "Communications Project" written in the center. Then, you could have four subcomponents named "social media, print advertising, mass emails, and video clips" each individually positioned north, east, south, and west off the main "Communications Project" circle.

✓ Thirdly, each of these subcomponents warrants its own brainstorming endeavors. For example, take "social media," and break it down into "channels, staffing, timing, and resources." These become sub-subcomponents that connect off from "social media." I have noticed that in continuing to map out my thoughts, other branches quickly emerge.

If managing a very intricate project, or studying a complex college course, the branches could continue to grow and fill the entire huge sheet of paper. Colored pens or pencils have become very helpful in distinguishing between various branches. Colored highlighters can allow the brainstorming team to put emphasis on important areas on the

map.

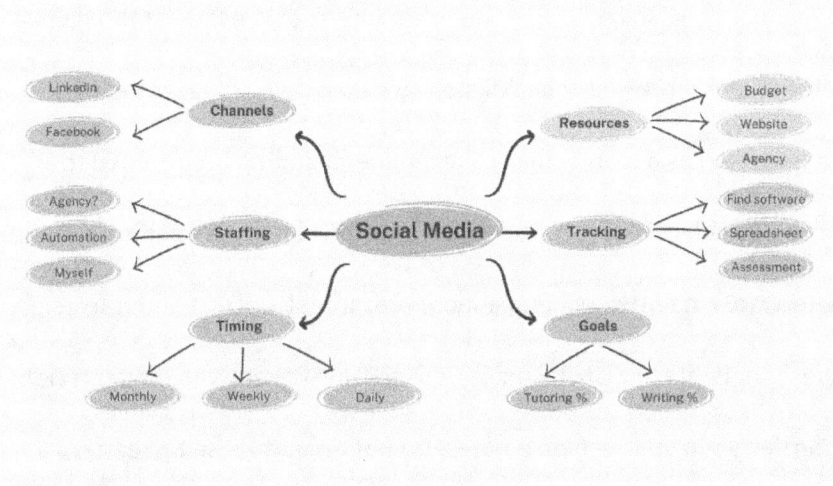

Yes, as you can imagine, this large resulting conglomerate of visually

depicted thoughts tells much on just one or a few pages. Test out

mapping your thoughts as you brainstorm an upcoming project or idea.

Personally, mapping thoughts and project ideas really inspires me to

squeeze the sponge and think creatively. It sharpens the innovation of a

team or small group gathered around collectively working on such a

map. Test it out!

Consider a personal, academic, or business project, and map out

your thoughts. Treat this as a journal entry. You can also test out

listening to another Ted Talk and mapping your thoughts.

I do both manual and digital mapping. Some maps work better using a manual style, so technology does not interrupt the flow of thoughts. Other maps work better in a digital style especially if presented to others, such as a team. Ideally, I recommend getting accustomed to both. Consider filling a desk pad full of your thoughts on a given subject. Afterwards, pair it down into a more presentable format and transfer these thoughts to a digital map. You can always keep the thoughts not transferred in your personal notes. Do not discard these too early in a project as you may need the extras, the thoughts that did not transfer to the digital map.

Additionally, many of the more sophisticated digital mapping tools allow for links. So, you might consider neatly typing up some bullet points or other form of documents and linking these off the thought tree. For example, a branch that reads as "Agency," when clicked upon could open a spreadsheet containing a list of potential agencies for consideration. In terms of a school project, a branch noting "Countries to consider" could link out to a list of countries. A science project that includes a test on the periodic table could link out to an actual picture of it. Also, digital thought maps can link to each other. So, a branch that reads, "Science" can link to a thought map for your science class. A branch that reads, "English" can link to a thought map for your English class. Expanding thought maps take on different shapes depending on the subject matter and the creative thought processes of the thinker. It should shift, mold, and develop according to your natural flow.

Outlining and Note Taking

My mind flashes back to personally learning the outlining method for the first time in church. Yes, you heard me, in church. I have a warm appreciation for the leaders who took time to pour into a small group of us young people. In a small country church, on several afternoons as I recall, youth leaders sat us down, gave us all our own personal "Spiritual Journey" notebooks, and began sharing all sorts of life lessons with us, one of which included how to take notes of the Bible study lessons taught by our youth leaders. They went on to share how to take notes on Sunday sermons shared by our pastor from the pulpit, and how to record our own personal discovery notes as we too began diving into the Bible. This period in my life still stands out as so amazingly life shaping. Back to note taking!

I learned from these dear people how to outline. As you will soon see, an outline makes use of seemingly easy steps. However, it does take some practice to really get the flow of it. I would say that over the years, outlining and thought mapping rank as my most frequent go to methods or recording thoughts and ideas.

Step 1: Start with a Title and heading. At the top of the paper or digital document, create a title and make note of the date and any other setting kinds of information, such as course number, workshop name, team meeting group, speaker name or author, etc.

Step 2: Identify the highest level of thought. For example, if learning about climate changes in different season in the United States, the highest level could include each of the seasons separately. One note of caution: Though you might identify this top level early, I recommend writing them more formally in the order that the notes will occur. So, at the beginning of the note taking process, I would only write "I. Winter." I am including the other seasons below to give you an idea of their appearance as each one comes up in the note taking process. These take on the roman numeral form and represent the highest level of thought for this note taking discussion.

I.   Winter
II.   Spring
III.   Summer
IV.   Fall

Subsequently, the teacher, the professor, or the independent learner

would explore variations found for the winter season. The second level

thoughts under "I. Winter" get recorded as upper-cased letters. A

second level thought representation might look something like the

following:

I.   Winter
       A. Weather and Climate
       B. Clothing and Comfort
       C. Notable Impact
II.   Spring
       A. Better Weather
       B. Lighter Clothing
       C. Better Economy
III.   Summer
       A. Mostly Sunny
       B. Beaches
       C. Tourism
IV.   Fall
       A. Windy
       B. Holidays and Festivities
       C. Schools

By now, you notice a pattern taking shape. Thoughts appear in

outline form quite organized. Subsequent layers continue falling

underneath the thoughts above. I have further developed out roman numeral I (one) as an example. Each of the roman numeral sections

could have more underlying layers. Normally, when arriving at the

bottom thought level for a given topic, I tend to express myself by

including a group of words, a phrase, or if needed, complete sentences.

I.   Winter
      A.   Weather and Climate
          1.   Northern states
              a.   Experience more snow and subzero weather.
              b.   Icy roads and sidewalks
          2.   Southern states
              a.   Varied weather rainstorms & some snow
              b.   Chilly weather, subzero not as frequent
              c.   Road conditions and sidewalks passable
      B.   Clothing and Comfort
          1.   Dressing in layers preferred
              a.   Northern states especially wear many layers of clothing.
              b.   Southern states may opt to carry extra top layers in case weather conditions change.
          2.   Fireplaces, heaters, warm drinks, soups
          3.   Indoor activities, family at home
      C.   Notable Impact
          1.   Traffic accidents in harsh weather conditions
          2.   Business and School Closures
          3.   Loss of life
          4.   Economic downturn

Summary

Listening and reading comprehension skills go hand in hand. Some

of the same attentiveness used while listening also applies to gaining a

higher reading comprehension level. In this next section, we will explore how to purposefully read in a way that yields the best outcomes. Before we dive into the techniques and tools to use in reading, we need to understand critical thinking.

Chapter Questions

1. If you have not created your own personal shorthand system, do so now. Next, pick the three favorite shorthand indicators from your list and share how frequently you anticipate using these in note taking. Test out taking notes using your shorthand system.

2. Review the Cornell note taking method. Design your own note taking template, test it out. Take notes and use your template. Did you notice any advantages or disadvantages to using your template? If so, can you think of anything to change? Going forward, will this template help you?

3. Test out note taking again. Keep using your shorthand system. Also, use your personal template and include at least one thought map. After finishing, look at this set of notes. Compare the notes you just took with prior ones. Explain any strengths or weaknesses. How could the use of thought maps aid your personal note taking effectiveness?

4. You have experimented with using a shorthand system, a note taking template, and at least one thought map. Identify your favorite combination and share any insights. Will such a combination help you store, retain, recall, and actively use the lesson contents – that which you took notes regarding?

5. Outlining can aid in organizing multiple layers of thought, such as found in formal lectures. It can also help in planning the writing of reports (addressed later in the book). Test out taking notes on a more complex subject. Use the outline method. Explain some of the takeaways. Identify any strengths or weaknesses you notice in using this method. Take the challenge. Test out combining all the methods together once again: shorthand system, note taking template, thought mapping, and outlining.

6. Which will you choose? Before heading on to the next chapter, decide which combination of note taking methods and tools you would like to use routinely. Explain your decision.

Section 4: Thinking and Studying

No doubt, you now have begun to think differently, more distinctly. Learning to listen and taking notes to aid memory does require patience and practice. Next, consider adding thinking and studying to this creative way of moving through life. It does make sense. If you benefited by learning how to listen better, then instructions on critical thinking and tips for studying will also prove helpful. I invite you to join me on a most delightful and interesting journey of all, one that dares to ask the question of how you think. What you consider important matters! These chapters should spark innovative and creative thinking. Additionally, studying will hopefully become more meaningful. Do not merely go through the motions. Add something; create something; evaluate things; and leave everything touched better than you find it. You deserve a chance to impact the world!

Activating critical thinking provides

the window frame to peer through

and to cultivate change

Chapter 9 Critical Thinking

Chapter Objectives

- Consider the societal impact of critical thinking. Explore how a student's thinking skills impact the future of even nations.

- Explore levels of learning as presented by the Bloom's Taxonomy model. Compare lower and high levels and gain an understanding of how students can perform better by choosing an upper level.

- Connect the dots by sharing how each generation can contribute to our society by thinking critically. Learn how younger and older generations can work together to arrive at better outcomes.

- Explore and think about your own thought processes and decide which cognitive levels of thought you reach. Challenge yourself to move to a higher level and yield better results.

- Contemplate and ponder using an incubation zone for thoughts and the processing of ideas. Brainstorm how to incorporate the process of incubation in your own studies.

In the last two chapters, we explored the subject of attentiveness and note taking. You learned some tips and techniques for paying attention and gained listening skills to improve focus. Attentiveness and note taking by themselves produce nothing more than scribbles and drawings on a page. In this chapter, we will go to the next level. What happens with the notes? Why did you pay attention? Why did you take that class in the first place? These questions do have a valid standing or appetite whetting place in education.

Getting the student to turn on and activate critical thinking skills lies at the very heart of educational goals. Utilizing such mental powers leads to innovation, creation, analysis, and application of learning. This sets the groundwork for lesson planning, curriculum development, and teacher education around the world. The goals rest on empowering students to make a difference. Activating critical thinking provides the window frame to peer through and to cultivate change.

I invite you to flip the script and consider learning from an educational theoretical perspective. By doing so, we can shed light on the direction to take and the best way to spark critical thinking.

Something New

Bloom's Taxonomy has shaped the course of education for many years.[5] The actual makeup and structure of the taxonomy has evolved or been rewritten by several in the education field. However, the

---

[5] (Armstrong 2010)

underlying core and rationale have remained the same. One major goal presented to educators, teachers, professors, and leaders has to do with "society contributions."

In layman's terms, "What can the student contribute to society upon completion of the education process?"

Critical thinking, at its best, results in something new being created: a new idea, an invention, new policies, or new operational procedures. This "newness" when poured into our societies and communities results in hopefully a better environment or community. Even in a family business, adding something "new" hopefully increases the longevity of the aspiring legendary business.

Knowing math and English does not create a thing! However, all learners start there and move up. The pinnacle of learning becomes inventing. Consider the following model to better understand this advancing educational growth concept.

Bloom's Taxonomy

The six levels of Bloom's Taxonomy consist of remembering, understanding, applying, analyzing, evaluating, and creating.

Remembering

At a **remembering** level, memorizing facts becomes one main goal. For example, a young child may be asked to recite the alphabet. A high school student may recite the periodic table. In either case, the work involved does not yet contribute to society. The student simply stores mental chunks of data in the brain.

Understanding

At an **understanding** level, explaining ideas and the meaning of things shows that the student has moved beyond a simple memorization level. Yet, even at this level, the person, no matter their age, has not truly contributed to society. They have simply utilized existing ideas and concepts.

Applying or Application

At an **applying or application** level, the understanding grows to a point where the student can use such ideas as intended, or as the originator of the concepts designed. This proves helpful in solving problems, in completing work projects, and in fixing broken items. One may argue that these actions do contribute to society. However, the

Blooms Taxonomy model sees these actions as not a new contribution, rather something already existing.

Analyzing

At an **analyzing** level, learners can perform "compare and contrast" thought processes in different situations. They can see relationships and make connections between various ideas and thoughts. Some argue, and I might agree, that this level should merge with the prior one. They fit so nicely together. In any case, fixing broken toys, analyzing how to do so, and comparing which way might work best, does not add newness to society. Yet, it does brush up against the coat sleeves of the next level. When comparing existing options using synthesis and analytical thought, often it naturally leads one to evaluation.

Evaluating

At the **evaluating** level, learners add in judgement. Something has become part of the learner's beliefs to the point that he or she can take a position or a stand. Argumentative essays, debate teams, and even thoughtful poetic writing can communicate how the learner feels about certain issues. Expressing one's beliefs in such a manner takes on an evaluating framework – one that assesses right from wrong, truth from lies, justice from injustice. However, even this high thinking level has not quite added value or newness to society. Someone can have a view or opinion about something, but it may not produce a newly created work. As one holds a belief strongly, perhaps after yielding time to such evaluative measures, a need for change often emerges, and courage propels a step into creating something different, something new.

Creating

The pinnacle level, **creating,** has its foundation on all the other levels. The learner rises to the occasion by taking personal beliefs, attitudes, a readily available application, an understanding of concepts, and knowledge of facts and creates something new, something that will hopefully add value and meaning in society. Creating uses ingenuity and equates to becoming a useful citizen, one that creates and adds value to our community.

Before proceeding, take some time and review the six levels. Think about your own experiences with learning. Which level do you tend to operate at most often? Which level do you find intriguing and interesting? Which level would you like to strive towards? Do you strive for the courageous stance required to innovate, to create? This does necessitate a need to step against the grain of common or to jump out of the bandwagon to new soil. It invites a lifestyle of pioneering and creating something unique. Write down your thoughts into a new journal entry before continuing onward.

Journal Entry – (Today's Date) – Which level interests you most?

Critical thinking differs from simply memorizing or obtaining a basic understanding of material. As people think critically, new ideas, thoughts, and inventions enter the distribution systems of our world. As you proceed towards dreams and your future, consider ways of adding value, consider the contributions you can make. Thinking critically along the way will help you in this endeavor. Certainly, just merely going along with the crowd, your peers, or your colleagues, will not put you into the realm of critical thinking and innovation. Instead, strive to turn on the light in the otherwise dark arena of an uncharted course – pioneer!

As you move forward, many times, projects, assignments, and regular work will at minimum require you to operate at one of the lower levels of Bloom's Taxonomy. While practicing critical thinking, and as you listen intently, be aware of everything in your toolbox. Challenge yourself to go higher, proceed richly, and enjoy the challenge of unturning new treasures.

Fully assess concepts, ideas, and problems. Additionally, discern the environment around you. Discern the cultures, the attitudes, and the intentions of those with whom you interact. Do not merely "go along with the crowd." Be encouraged to take it all in, assess fully, evaluate appropriately, and decide to agree or disagree with whatever has already been presented. If you ever find yourself not agreeing with the crowd, then if warranted, create something new. Be bold! Be adventurous! Stand up and add value, add newness, and reach the pinnacle of learning – CREATE!

Take some time now and record your thoughts. Critical thinking inspires creative thinking. How do these things benefit society? What can you contribute? What can you create? Will you challenge yourself?

Journal Entry – (Today's Date) – Does creative forms of thinking benefit society?

From Generation to Generation

With each generation, new ideas, inventions, and ways of doing things emerge. You do need to honor those who have taught you. Honor and respect those who have already traveled the road ahead. Creating does not equate to merely "throwing out the baby with the bath water." Creating something new requires taking the treasured learning already obtained and transforming, shaping, recreating in a way that produces value. Having worked and led a very innovative team for many years, I share these words of wisdom with you.

Treasure and honor the gifts of learning given by those who have carefully poured into you. Use your skills, abilities, insights, new tools, advancements, creative thought, and critical thought to do more. Yet, show respect and kindness. As you test out new ideas, start small. You will want to pilot these ideas first. Test them on a smaller scale, perhaps with just a few people. If it works beautifully on a small scale, consider expanding gradually. Testing on a smaller scale will allow you to adjust before implementing your new ideas enterprise or business wide.

Repeatedly, I have found that piloting with a smaller crew first does uncover a need to revise, to tweak, to change course. Additionally, containing eager excitement, and advancing on a project with more cautious intervals of successful testing leads to less costly implementation. Afterall, if a project team rolls out a new solution to a problem before fully testing it, then that solution may not work when applied to various environments. Thus, the funds spent on seeing the solution deployed prematurely become wasted.

Therefore, I encourage you to courageously come up with new inventions, new innovations to solve problems. Yet, also make sure to maintain self-control, self-discipline, patience, and skillfully test your idea step by step before having others take part on a wider scale. As you do so, keep a log or journal of things you learn along the way. These lessons learned will prove invaluable for your future. Use these inciteful lessons learned along the way to help in planning out future innovations and explorations.

You, the next generation, yes you can add value. Just do so with care, with thoughtfulness, and passion. Continue marching forward to reach dreams, to accomplish what your mind and heart envision, and to add a great deal of value to our communities. Always do your best to show consideration for people around you. Be patient as everyone does not process or think alike. It takes time for others to understand new approaches, new innovations, and proposed changes to the current flow or way of life.

In this next journal entry, you will take time to reflect on how people from all different generations contribute to the good of society. Do you believe each generation has something to add, or should the newest generation simply start a new, using the latest and greatest technologies and resources? Take time to record your thoughts before proceeding.

Journal Entry – (Today's Date) – Generation to generation

Congratulations on getting this far through the book. I must admit to having written that last portion with watery eyes. I cheer you onward. You do help shape even my future. The things that you choose to put your time into from this point forward will shape your future and that of people around you. May you choose wisely. Plan from the mind but also follow your heart. In my case, being of Christian orientation, I follow God's leading. I ask Him to shape my heart and lead my thoughts. I ask Him to direct my feet and my hands in the best way to add value to this place in which we live today, this place called earth. I ask Him to pour through me, to touch and change the world. Let's together make this a better place!

The incubator
Critical thinking often requires time. Waiting to study until the night before a big test, one that involves complex concepts, can prove

disastrous. I have experienced such a tragedy firsthand, one that resulted in me dropping a college class in my undergraduate days long ago. Instead of providing time and space for dwelling on, pondering, and wrestling with the subject matter, I chose to defrost the freezer. Yes, this dates me somewhat. This freezer did not have the automatic defrost features that we have today. Such a process, chipping away at ice and patiently maneuvering the cold chunks until they would fall off the edges of the inner sides of the freezer took away precious time. Yes, I bombed the test and opted to drop that class. I imagine everyone does make mistakes during their early college days. However, learn the concept of incubation. In so doing, save yourself from some pitfalls.

Normally, people think of incubators when it comes to watching baby chicks hatch from eggs. After the hen lays her eggs, the hatching does not happen overnight. I remember watching such little chicks. Did you know that it takes about three weeks for the baby chick to emerge from the egg. That last bit, the getting its body into position, then bit by bit pecking through the shell takes energy and commitment on the part of the baby chick.

When new information, such as that assigned by your teacher, gets deposited inside of your brain. It often requires time before the meat of the learning materials process fully. You receive it best using multisensory receptors. Your eyes, ears, and fingers receive the new data. Mentally pondering, thinking about, and meditating on this new stuff creates change.

Change, that as noted earlier, could stay at an "understanding" level or propel upward to a "create" one. The likelihood of advancing to a creative level remains slim if no dedicated efforts get applied to the mix. Rushing through homework, rapidly finishing, and not really focusing and going in deep on the matter robs students of so much more. An incubation stage in learning refers to the process of letting new information reside in your focus, your attention, long enough to apply your opinion, formulate beliefs, and possibly creatively explore new territory.

Creative people often live many hours each week inside this incubational realm of learning. I challenge you to go deeper, think outside of the box, and critically focus and think about each subject ahead.

For many, a special place, or a special time of day, and perhaps a certain musical instrumental background – these all contribute to the learning environment. What sparks your learning excitement and adventure? Where do you like to hang out? Do you sip on your favorite tea or coffee? Do you have background music playing? Do you study best at a certain time of day? Find your incubation zone. Find the combination that best suits you. Then, make sure to schedule the time to study with these considerations in mind. Take a few minutes to jot down some thoughts about your incubation environment.

Journal Entry – (Today's Date) – My Best Incubation Environment

---

Side note: If you do listen to background music, make sure to monitor how it impacts studies. I find that non-sleepy instrumental music works best for me. If the songs have words, then that throws off my focus.

Summary

The ways you think about life, the world around you, and day-to-day questions and decisions continue to develop and mature. Maturity in thinking critically can emerge by identifying level markers along the Bloom's Taxonomy continuum. Thinking at the higher levels, such as analyzing and creating, holds the greatest potential for inspiring change. Educators and leaders seek to equip students and participants to think at a higher level and to create new ideas and innovations that will positively impact the world in which we live. As a student or learner, grasping an understanding and challenging yourself to function on a higher critical thinking level often results in performing better in school and in the workforce. In the upcoming chapter, we will explore how to add study techniques to further assist you in organizing thoughts and retaining materials.

Chapter Questions

1. In this chapter, you learned about Bloom's Taxonomy. Take some time now and list out each of the levels mentioned. Next to each level, take some notes. Thinking through your most recent personal study session, at which levels did you operate? Explain your answer.

2. How can functioning at an upper level of thinking change society? Can you contribute to your community by challenging yourself?

3. How can a student's grades in school improve by thinking at a higher level? Will you test this out for yourself? How can you make use of this new knowledge?

4. Explain the dangers of throwing out old approaches for a new way of doing things. How can generations benefit from working together?

5. Explain what it means to incubate ideas or thoughts. Share how this process can help produce better results. Can you think of a time in which you allowed an idea to incubate? Share how the idea turned out. Did allowing time for incubating help?

I find that diving in deeply,

exploring fully, and developing an

art for questioning, investigating,

imploring, and learning, has

required much courage.

Chapter 10 Subject Choice and Study Habits

Chapter Objectives

- Discover how knowing your sweet spot can help you when selecting classes.

- Identify the pitfalls of only studying well in classes you love.

- Check your heart by comparing your attitude and motivation towards studying different subjects.

- Describe each letter of the acronym SQ3R.

- Apply SQ3R in a manner that results in an improvement to your study habits and an increase in the retention of materials.

- Exercise the 4Ps of preparing ahead of time using a proven study method.

- Explore ways to improve your class participation while stepping into new territory.

- Discover ways to improve your focus even in noisy settings.

Course Selection

Proceeding forward in their studies, students enroll in a variety of classes. As noted earlier, some of these classes bring with them joy and excitement, while others may not be quite so pleasing. Regardless of whether you like the list of classes appearing on next semester's schedule, something remains true, you will want to do well in your studies.

Should you get opportunity to select the classes in the future, remember your "sweet spot." Take time to recall it from the "Your Personal Discovery" chapter presented earlier. Do you remember your dreams for the future? Read through your journal entries. Review what you have already included in your personal portfolio, and remind yourself of the missing key elements, those things you wish to learn. See the chapter on "Portfolio Creation and Show Case," and read the journal entries that you wrote for that chapter. Now, looking through the possible courses to take for the next school semester or quarter, which ones best fit? Which one could propel you forward towards a nice future? If given the opportunity to select the professor or instructor to sit under for the class in question, do your research.

Perhaps the school has some biographical information available, maybe your institution has "meet the professors" available, or peers give insights. Could you sit in one of their classes? Especially if paying tuition, do well on your investment, and choose the best instructors. Even if you have no such freedom, do not lose hope. You will have the materials available, and with proper care, dedication, and work, diving into the subjects ahead could prove rather rewarding.

Heart and Attitude Check

After selecting the classes, you will want to tune up on study skills, especially when heading to high school and college. How you study makes a difference in grades received and in the retention of what you learn. Study methods can help no matter if learning dull subjects, complex interesting ones, or ones that involve lengthy materials. The way you study can help regardless of how talented your instructor or professor may appear. It even helps if you have never received high marks before. First, get your footing, gain some connectivity to the subject.

Sometimes, new ground may seem uninteresting because of personal lack of connectivity. Have you ever studied this subject before? In general, many people feel uneasy when presented with something brand new to learn. However, by the time you have become more familiar with the new subject and have mastered it enough to take tests and score well in class, it may turn out to be your favorite subject of choice!

It really happened that way in my case. I signed up for a computer programming class during my undergraduate college years. The challenging class assignments resulted in many sleepless nights, and it offered little time to socialize with friends, and left me feeling a bit inadequate! Looking back at that first main experience with computer technology, I see that it did discourage me, mostly because of not really having anything like that class before. I felt fearful, intimidated, and thought I had gotten myself into something too hard for me. After the class ended, I did not want to touch the computer again. "Never again!" I announced to my roommates. This era in my life came prior to having a keen use of study skills. I helplessly plodded my way through. No, I did not carefully read the textbook or study the class notes. I thought that would take too long! I laugh now. Really? Of course, I would have slept more and enjoyed the class if I had carefully studied.

Fortunately, circumstances changed along the way. Can you believe it? I ended up in that field as a career! So, do not be discouraged if you find yourself not doing well on something the first time you explore a particular area of study. Take comfort in knowing two things: (1) you will improve, and (2) most fields of study have a wide variety within them. So, try the same field from a different angle. Though I worked for many

116

years in a technological field, I discovered a joy for the parts that include people and computers together, rather than just programming. Yes, you will encounter various difficulties in the subjects placed before you. Maybe like me, you may find yourself apprehensive about studying and preparing for tests. Travel on to explore one of my favorite study methods that proved most helpful.

The SQ3R Study Method

SQ3R has gained a great deal of popularity over the years.[6] It certainly has revolutionized how students choose to study and how they retain materials. In a nutshell, SQ3R turns the learner into a teacher. So, even if you did not land the most brilliant teacher, this method, if embraced fully, will help you soar and dive into the deep depths of the subject.

Welcome! First, you must choose to require self-discipline of yourself and to set aside time for careful study. If studying has not really been your thing before, I encourage you to really lean in, put aside the past, and set sight for the future. You will create the self-tests and the

---

[6] (Robinson 1946)

study routine. Welcome to SQ3R! Please do not rush through the exploration of this section. You will want to test out every step of this process and own it!

This has the potential to reframe and change your perspective on studying. While this book offers no money back guarantees or warranties, SQ3R's popularity speaks for itself. When properly applied, this method works extremely well!

The Steps

First, please select a textbook, preferably something that reflects the level of reading required for your future. Review the table of contents, read through any introductory information, and turn pages throughout the book to get a taste of it. Next, turn to chapter 1 to begin the SQ3R process.

S Stands for Survey

Find and **thoughtfully and carefully read** the following from your textbook. Resist the temptation to read everything. Read these pieces instead:

o   Chapter title

o   Chapter objectives (Note: Objectives often end up on tests!)

- o First sentence of each major paragraph

- o Subheadings

- o Bold print terms

- o Read definitions.

- o Look at charts, diagrams, and pictures.

- o Note anything else that stands out.

Do not read the entire chapter.

Wait! Scanning or surveying builds your anticipation, increases curiosity, and whets the appetite for reading more. It also sketches a mental preview of the artistic landscape just ahead.

After performing the "S – Survey" step, you have an idea of what this chapter will cover. Hopefully, you also have questions, "What is a

_____?" Fill in the blanks. That feeling of questioning goes with you into the next step. Ideally, before closing the book, move on to completing the question step immediately following the survey one. If time passes, then perhaps do the survey again prior to continuing.

Q Stands for Questions

You now have a vague understanding of the content of the chapter. Also, hopefully, the survey step sparked some curiosity and raised questions in your mind.

Take out your journal book and create a new entry. Go back through and make a list of questions to go with this chapter. <u>Do not include any answers, only questions.</u>

Journal Entry – (Today's Date) – SQ3R Question Step Practice – Chapter 1

Book Title: (Your book's title)

These tips will get you started:

o   Turn the title into an overall question. For example, if the title reads, "Space Pollution," you may write, "Describe space pollution and explain how it got there."

o   Turn each objective into one or more questions.

o   Turn each subheading into a question.

o   Turn each bold print term into a question.

o   Charts, pictures, and diagrams can also become points for questions.

o   Anything else that prompted curiosity turns into questions too.

At this point, breathe! Many students have expressed a sense of feeling overwhelmed by the number of questions and the time involved in capturing running thoughts. Again, refocus, ground yourself in some basic truths.

The 4Ps

- **Pieces** - First, the subject contains details worth remembering.
- **Practice** - Secondly, you master knowing all from a comprehensive test bank with practice.
- **Peace** - Thirdly, dealing with the emotions and feelings associated with not knowing the answers quite yet now will prepare you in advance for conquering the actual in class tests. SQ3R does take some practice.
- **Progress** - However, it does help students make their way to the top of their class.

Now, with questions in hand, travel on to the exploration step, and have fun discovering so many new things. Enjoy and step forward into the learning adventure!

R Stands for Read

You may have already guessed. We need some answers to all those questions. Before you begin reading the chapter, gain some understanding of how to read textbooks. Textbook reading has a very different feel than simply reading a novel or fictional storybook.

Many students fall asleep reading textbooks because they do not read with intentionality and purpose. Attending night classes, working while going to school, and having other responsibilities all add up to students having busy schedules. Most students report having to stay up late or get up early to engage in their studies. No wonder everyone falls asleep! To help with this dilemma, carry out the SQ3R "R" step.

Read to find the answers to the questions you listed earlier. As you find these answers, write them down. You will want to record them on an "Answer Sheet." Do not mix questions with answers. Questions only go on the Question Sheet, and answers go on the Answer Sheet. Create a new journal entry and test this out.

You will now read the chapter and create the answer key. Keep the same numbering method as you had for the question list. So, answer number one should correspond with question number one. Find the answers to each question listed earlier. Some questions may require you to ponder and think more deeply. So, allow yourself plenty of time.

Did you find answers to all the questions? Most likely, you came up with a couple of questions that appear to have no available answers. Do not throw away these questions. Bring them to class! Most teachers and professors award a few points for participation. Some reward higher participations points for students who do ask questions in class. These unanswered questions provide ground for the teacher or professor to shine and for your course grade to improve.

Always show kindness and respect when asking questions. Also, discern whether the class has enough time for your questions. Remember to record the answers relayed by your teacher or professor on your Answer Sheet. Additionally, some questions that yield no answers may signal an area for potential innovation, for pioneering, and for stepping into a new territory. Before heading into the next letter, "R" for Recite, I have something to share with you.

The Art of Learning

I do need to pause for a moment and give some wise warning ahead of time. As you really go deep into SQ3R, professors and teachers do tend to notice. However, other peers, the students around you do too. Many students bring to class their own feelings of inadequacy and lack of self-respect. Sadly, in our society today, feelings of depression, lack of confidence, envy, jealousy, and even bullying exist around us. You may have already encountered such things and experienced firsthand seeing these weaknesses in students in your classes.

In a fast paced, highly competitive world, people who do not know any better may believe that putting others down and stomping out competitor successes will work best. Such individuals may even feel it helps them propel and rise while defeating others along the way. Of course, this runs counter intuitive to the truth.

Working together, promoting, and applauding progress, and cheering with delight when witnessing greatness, helps one's own advancement. What does this have to do with SQ3R? Everything! As you step forward to ask the "unanswerable" questions, ones you personally raised during study times, ones that perhaps even your professors and instructors have not thought of before, others do notice. Other people around you might start whispering. In my own experience, when asking intriguing questions of my professors, some stopped their entire lecture, and pondered. Then, the lecture board got totally filled with their expressions and thoughtful answers. Sometimes, such thoughts and questions even landed on subsequent classroom tests.

These lectures delighted me! In some ways, such responses fueled my desire to learn even more. It often transformed an otherwise boring lecture into an exploration, full of lively discussions and new thoughts. However, some students certainly did not appreciate my desire to know more. I had to learn to calm such urges inside of me that would want to verbally lash out at these quaint individuals. Now, years later, I realize that many of those who may express discontent with innovation and forward-thinking struggle inwardly. Their words, though directed at my insights and questions raised, do not really have anything to do with me personally, rather, they just highlight the individual's own problems.

I find that diving in deeply, exploring fully, and developing an art for questioning, investigating, imploring, and learning, has required much courage. It does take great determination and commitment. Yet, the classes and explorations that I have truly treasured highly, end up being the ones in which differences between individuals get set aside, and in an SQ3R style, with everything that I am -- my heart and mind -- I embrace learning, and do so with other bright and talented individuals.

Why do I enjoy teaching so much? I love the continual learning experience gained when engaging with students who also welcome such adventures! Keep learning! Continue the race of growing and exploring. In doing so, you add so much to your own life and to the world.

Ask yourself a question. Will you exercise the boldness and courage to press forward? Will you present the unasked questions? Will you embrace the art of learning? Record your thoughts in response to these questions.

Journal Entry – (Today's Date) – How Will I Embrace Learning?

Before continuing to read the next portion of SQ3R, practice the proceeding steps. Become comfortable, then move on to the "R – Recite" testing phase.

Test Yourself

Hopefully, you have gone through the survey, question, and read steps, and now we will look at the next step, recite. As you take part in this one, imagine that your instructor or professor has prepared a test for you! Are you ready?

R Stands for Recite

Put away your textbook. Do not look at the answers. Put those away too! Practice these steps in your journal book. While normally, in the future, you will most likely be using loose leaf college lined notebook paper instead, I encourage you to record everything in your journal book for the first attempt. This will ensure you have personal notes recorded on how to do the SQ3R steps. These will come in handy in the future.

You will now attempt to answer all the questions found on the Question page of your journal. Again, you do not want to record any answers on the same page as these questions. Keep all answers separate. For our practice, please create a new journal entry. Make sure to indicate "TRY #1" in the heading and put the date of this first attempt.

You will simulate taking a quiz or test covering the material just read. Make sure to write the question number next to each of your attempted answers. Even if you have forgotten the answer, put something for each number. Take a guess! Do not write the questions.

Simply, write your guesses and thoughts for the answers.

Journal Entry – (Today's Date) – SQ3R Recite Step Practice – Chapter 1 – TRY #1

Book Title: (Your book's title)

Anticipation Deserves a Break

Take at least a 15-minute break after you finish guessing all the answers. In a real class setting, you normally do not get the graded quiz, test, or exam back immediately. The break simulates that suspense and that feeling of wanting to know how you did. Initially, many students fight feelings of inadequacy.

"I should have studied longer! I got half of these questions wrong! Why do I have to take this class?"

If this sounds like you, rewrite the mental script! As you embark on a whole new way of studying, remain hopeful, patient, and determined. Tell yourself a new message.

Repeat this out loud:

"I will master this before the actual test. Practicing repeatedly until I can achieve a high score assures me of confidence on the test. My question sheets look much more complete than the test in class. Not only will I ace the real one, but this will also give me the chance to learn well. I can do this! I will be patient!"

After taking a nice break of at least fifteen minutes, continue to the next step of the SQ3R process. You will become proficient at this over a longer period. Remember, a good learner also becomes a great teacher! Step into that role now – both learner and teacher.

Scoring and Review

Yes, it may feel painful at first. Where do you stand? Do you fully understand the material?

R Stands for Review

Adjust the recipe! Think of it this way. If a chef merely prepared great entrees without even sampling the results, he would not have a way of knowing what to adjust. The review step provides a chance to taste your level of understanding. An excellent cook will experiment, sample along the way, and even prepare the dish multiple times. In doing so, the recipe gets perfected and eventually the dish gets served in fancy cafes or restaurants. See your study area as the kitchen. You must assess progress and continue practicing!

The third R in SQ3R stands for Review. After returning from your break, take out everything: the textbook, the questions, the correct answers, and your "TRY #1" guesses. Also, you will want a red pen for grading. Yes, grade your TRY #1. If you have a question wrong, mark a big red X over the number. Then, write in the correct answer. This will help you learn the material even more. Do not stop simply at placing the red X. You must write the correct answer.

When you finish marking up the try sheet, use your calculator, and give yourself a percentage grade. If you got 45 correct out of 50 possible questions, then 45 divided by 50 would result in a grade of 90%. You will want to repeat the recite and review process until reaching 100%. However, I have found it works best to allow at least a few hours to pass before trying again. If you did not do well, schedule time to repeat the process. Deliberately prepare for the upcoming tests.

Do not skip class. Afterall, if you skip class, then how will you receive the added insights from your teacher or professor? Even if classmates offer their notes, this too proves inadequate.

Appending to the Question-and-Answer Sheets

In earlier chapters, we discussed the importance of class notes. Make sure to also go through your class notes and add questions to your question sheet. Add answers to your answer sheet. Teachers and professors often add material during class that does not appear anywhere in the textbook. You will need to diligently work at keeping your question list current. You will add more questions with each chapter assigned for reading. You will add more questions for each day's class notes. Yes, your own test, the one personally designed, will end up being more complete than that administered by the teacher or professor.

As you write answers on the answer sheet, I recommend incorporating diagrams, thought maps, formulas, and other visual reminders. Your goal includes creating the most complete question bank possible, then learning the material well.

Location, Location, Location

As a young undergraduate at the University of Texas, another challenge to test taking came to me in the form of distractions. Fellow students making a variety of noises would easily annoy me. Despite studying ahead of time, unknowingly, such inward frustrations would result in my attention being diverted to the various sounds rather than to the test at hand. Students with their pencils tapping, desks and chairs scooting along the floor, sniffles and sneezes, coughs and whispers, and any variety of paper shuffling would instantly thwart my progress. Sometimes, I would even express myself out loud, "Shhhhhh please!"

I guess in some ways, my inner working self does have sensory wiring. Attentive to sounds, tastes, and visual happenings can help in other scenarios. However, in taking tests, I found that these input mechanisms needed some special refinement.

Over the years, listening to many students sharing their own frustrations, I have learned that most students do experience some level of challenge in dealing with distractions. If you can relate to all of this, I have good and bad news to share. First, unfortunately, you cannot make all the distractions cease; after all, people continue to act like people – not robots. Many make noise! However, you can proactively prepare your mind and emotions to sit through such distractions and to turn your attention back to the test at hand. This skill, if properly developed, will serve you well throughout life. Even now, this day, as I write the book, I must block out the distractions around me and focus on sharing my thoughts with you.

The future ahead of you will hold many distractions along the way. As a student, noise during a test provides a learning ground to prepare you for the road ahead. In a career setting, when sitting behind an office desk, distractions commonly abound. Office chatter, cleaning staff attending to neatness, visitors entering, vendors promoting products, colleagues stopping by to ask questions, friends inquiring about lunch appointments, invitations to attend meetings, phones ringing, email notifications popping up, noisy equipment rolling down the nearby hallway or outside the windowpane, and a wide variety of sounds bid for attention. If you get easily distracted, be encouraged, and read on!

To prepare for taking your test amidst distractions, and to practice for the future, consider your study environment. I do believe in studying in a quiet space when going through most of the SQ3R steps. However, I learned the secret. At least for me, moving around, trying different spots, and simulating sitting in a noise filled environment proves most helpful when working through the "R – Recite" step.

Do add a huge amount of patience to the equation. I remember my own self-criticisms piled on when first attempting such a change. I really did lousy! At first, I missed most of the questions. However, I felt incredibly grateful that the simulated zones gave me much opportunity to discipline my mind and steady my emotions. As I repeated the process, and even added a clicking timer to the setup, over time, the skill of mental focus developed greatly! Today, I can even type this chapter with a variety of sounds simultaneously going on around me. Do sounds throw you off course? Do you get annoyed at all the surrounding sounds when taking a test? When you study, do sounds bother you? Start slowly but come up with some different settings for practicing the recite step.

Next, time yourself. Some tests must be completed within a certain time limit. Think of the classroom in which you anticipate taking the real test. Can you think of a place to sit that might have some of the same kinds of sounds? Can you add some type of timing device?

Take some time to jot down your own thoughts and experiences. Do you get distracted during tests? What distracts you? How does this impact your test? What type of environment could you simulate for test taking practice? Where could you sit?

Journal Entry – (Today's Date) – Test Taking Distractions

Above all, be patient with yourself. Sensitivity to sounds most of the time equates to a very good trait, so do not lose that all the way. Just learn to tweak it for the situation at hand. Over time, you will develop some very nice skills! Keep practicing without becoming discouraged. What floats your boat? Do you study better for classes that interest you? Or do you exercise the same level of discipline for the courses that do not look very interesting?

Attitude and Heart Check

Before proceeding, take time to uncover any roadblocks. Consider a set of classes you have already completed or perhaps ones in progress. Create a new journal entry to record your response.

Journal Entry – (Today's Date) – Attitude and Heart Check

- Make a list of the courses.
- Next, rate your joy and excitement level for each class. On a scale from 1 to 10, how excited do you feel about each one? (1 = low and 10 = high)

- Next, ask yourself to rate the level of study diligence for each class. Do you study consistently or wait until little time remains? Rate your personal commitment and effort level on a scale from 1 to 10. Place your ratings next to the earlier one.

- Finally, ask yourself how effective your study approach has turned out so far. Have you retained (remembered) the materials? Have you scored well in class? Next to the other two ratings, give yourself an "effectiveness" rating from 1 to 10.

Do you see any patterns? Challenge yourself to keep the joy for learning high. Most people easily commit to putting in the effort and doing their best if the class looks appealing. However, flipping the script can change things. This change begins with developing an attitude that willingly embraces even the most foreign or bewildering subjects head on.

Having the best attitude will take you further in your studies and in life. Determine to excel! Determine to overcome obstacles. Learn! Learn and learn some more. Then, with an eager heart, innovate – change and create. Once you clothe your heart and mind with the right attitude and way of thinking, acquiring top study skills will help you do well.

Summary

Study with intentionality. Planning to simply read through a text without any method for retaining the materials often leads students to score poorly in their classes. In this chapter, you have explored techniques for staging your studies and improving your grades. SQ3R and the 4Ps, when properly applied, will help you establish a solid studying framework.

Chapter Questions

1. Have you ever felt disappointed? Why does studying quickly or at the last minute not produce the best results?

2. How can knowing your sweet spot help you when selecting courses to take?

3. Having read this chapter, can you identify at least one or two pitfalls to only doing your best on courses you love? Explain.

4. Can you now explain the meaning of each letter SQ3R?

5. How can focusing your attention on SQ3R personally help you?

6. List the 4Ps mentioned in this chapter. How do these differ from the approaches you have tried in the past?

7. Does it take boldness to tackle the unanswered question? Explain.

8. Can class attendance impact a student's study habits? Explain.

9. Why should you take a break before grading your self-test?

10. How can distractions hinder test taking? What can you do to help improve focus in such a case?

11. Did you find any nice takeaways in this chapter? What will you personally do, moving forward?

Section 5: Word Power

For this section, I have included a bridge the gap chapter. Having come across students who secretly struggle with phonics, the very next chapter seeks to help bridge gaps. Should you not need such assistance, please feel free to skip over this one and proceed to chapter 10. Developing a comfort in using words will help improve many aspects of life: reading, writing, and conversations. Nothing feels more embarrassing than finding yourself at a loss for words. The prior section sparked creative and innovative thinking. Proceeding forward, building your vocabulary will help you express ideas and thoughts clearly. I have put together some fun tips for growing your vocabulary. My students have tested out these tips and exercises and found them useful. I am sure you will soon benefit from learning new words and communicating more confidently.

Putting it all together, exploration

means to go "out" + "explore" +

"perform a process." Exploration is the

process of going out and exploring.

Chapter 11 Bridging the Gap-Word Start

Chapter Objectives

- Discover foundational phonics and set personal goals towards developing pronunciation and spelling proficiencies.

- Establish a stronger foundation in writing and pronouncing consonants and vowels.

- Solidify sounds associated with combining two or more letters together.

- Grow comfortable with assessing word syllables and exploring word cues, like pronunciations and definitions.

- Journey through an exploration of prefixes, roots, and suffixes, and increase vocabulary power through routine practice.

I have had the joy of helping many students face their hesitations and fears of weaknesses in reading and vocabulary, so I get it. No, everyone does not come into the world, born with "word genius." At birth, all babies start with knowing zero words. Yes, everyone starts somewhere on the journey to discover and learn new words.

A Baby's World

Given the vastness of our world, the population at large has experienced a whole variety of learning experiences. Inside the family system, young children become enticed by hopefully loving adults and older siblings to communicate. The language spoken in the home gets infiltrated into any new arriving babes. Many even grow accustomed to a multi-language culture. I believe such realities, for the most part help children develop a rich vocabulary.

The Struggle to Catch Up

Eventually, under normal circumstances, children go to school or perhaps take up private instruction at home. Kids interact with peers, and under the supervision and teaching of an adult learn phonics, word formation, and begin the process of growing their vocabulary banks. Tragically, this process does not go as smoothly for many young pupils. For a variety of circumstances, some uncontrollable, the child may have either skipped entire fundamental word development portions of instruction or simply have been thrust into such a process prematurely. In either case, this student now grins and bears with a "catch up" struggle that could last a lifetime.

So, at the onset of a discussion on word power, I have decided to briefly address such an audience. First, I applaud you for even picking up this book, because surely reading it has so far proven very difficult. Next, I want you to understand that you can catch up. My eyes have witnessed this in other students, and if you do apply certain techniques to bridge word building gaps, it will help decrease frustrations in approaching new words. Students who persistently stay motivated and consistently practice, yield better results. Take a few minutes, and with determination, ask yourself two questions. First, what kinds of things continue to hold you back in terms of writing and English skills? Secondly, what goals could you set today, and how would your life look like upon reaching these?

Journal Entry – (Today's Date) Presentation Goals

Bridging Gaps – A Look at Letters

Take time to carefully inspect the English alphabet. Carefully say the entire alphabet. Do you know the sounds for each letter? At the time of this writing, many resources exist online to help with brushing up on the proper sounds for the alphabet letters. Some students secretly struggle with confusing the sounds of letters. For example, the letter "c" sometimes sounds like the letter "s" while at other times it may sound like the letter "k." Some students, having learned the alphabet at a very young age, initially confused the shapes of letters, such as "b" versus "d" or "m" versus "n." This confusion, having become engrained in some mental thought processes, has contributed to problems associated with illiteracy, or at the very least, difficulties with approaching new words. If you can relate to anything I just shared, check out the online resources by browsing the internet for phonics development. I may write a separate book on the subject should time permit. In the meantime, a vast array of materials already exists. One word of encouragement and caution to note as you set out to peruse phonics, do not discount or skip materials written for a younger audience. The materials written for younger students have for the most part been presented in simple terms, which might leave an older audience feeling somewhat insulted. Flip the script by realizing that as an older student, you should fly more quickly through these resources. So, be encouraged to take a step in the right direction by diving into phonetic development exercises.

Bridging the Gap – Vowels

The next step in improving comfortability with word power has to do with vowels. You most likely know all the English vowels: a, e, I, o, u, and sometimes y. Many students stopped simply after reciting these beautiful letters. Did you know that each of these vowels have short and long sounds? Do you know the short and long sounds? If not, take time to review these again by browsing the online resources readily available on the internet. Make sure to gain a good understanding of these differences because doing will improve your ability to sound out and pronounce new words.

Bridging the Gap – Put Letters Together

After becoming more comfortable with individual letters, the next step in increasing confidence with words has to do with the sounds associated with putting two letters together. For example, in English we have blend sounds; "b" and "r" by themselves sounds different than "br" placed side by side. Browse the online resources and explore phonetic blends. Explore the other various two and three letter combinations associated with English phonics. Though I am not including them here, these resources exist across the internet. If you do have phonetic gaps in understanding words, set a goal and practice every day on these basics. If you feel embarrassed, many students confess feeling this way, find a private place and practice daily. Just make it a point to practice consistently each day, and over just a few weeks, the problems that have plagued you will decrease. Word power does not have to feel so painful and frustrating. Additionally, remove all the negative labels. As an older student now, with the ability to understand more, you can learn at a much faster rate. You can fill in these personal learning gaps. Taking care to devote time over a few weeks will change your future!

Bridging the Gap – Dissecting the words

If you have reached this juncture as one attempting to catch up, to fill in elementary level gaps, working with word syllables could quickly help. Grab hold of your chin and say a word such as "exploration." Yes, you most likely know the meaning of the word, but what a great place to start. Say the word again, and this time carefully count the number of times your chin moves. Did you count four movements of the chin? This word has exactly four syllables. Test it out! Take a list of random words and practice syllable counting. Each time your chin moves denotes the beginning of a new syllable. If you place small dots or dashes or a separator at these positions, that will set the word up for further dissection.

Ex – plor – a – tion

While you could look the word exploration up in the dictionary, doing so might slow down a good read of your favorite book. Certainly, dictionaries do provide great information, and we do need to continue using them. However, becoming familiar with common word parts could help the reader narrow down the word's meaning rather quickly. So, how could one begin such a journey?

Bridging the Gap - Prefixes

Go to your favorite internet browser and key in "free word prefix lookup" in the search bar. Take time to explore. Look up "ex" in the finder. We find the prefix at the beginning of a multi-syllable word. "Ex" is the prefix in the word exploration. Looking up this prefix, reveals that it means "out" or something that has passed. This same prefix exists in so many common and not so common words. The dentist extracts teeth by taking them **out.** We go on an exploration by traveling **outside**. We may even go **out** to exercise.

By browsing the internet, you should find a list of prefixes. Now, go back and search the internet for common word prefixes. Find a nice prefix list and begin memorizing and learning the meanings of the common prefixes. I have included just a few here to get you started.

Commit these prefixes to memory. Begin noticing words that begin with these prefixes.

Prefix	Meaning	Prefix	Meaning
anti-	against	non-	not
auto-	self	poly-	many
dis-	not	pre-	before
ex-	out, past	re-	again
fore-	prior	semi-	half
im-	without	sub-	under
in-	not	trans-	across
ir-	not	tri-	three
mis-	wrong	un-	not

Bridging the Gap – Root words

The English language consists of many words that have come over to America from different countries or they got added to the dictionary during different periods of time. Studying root word origination points could improve vocabulary understanding and increase your proficiency in spelling. Though diving deeply into the root words, or the main part of a multiple syllable word is beyond the scope of this book, be encouraged. Browse the internet for "common root words in the English language." Many of our root words have a Latin or Greek origin. At this time of this writing, one nice resource is that found at the www.YourDictionary.com website.[7] Go to this site, find the Knowledge section, and search for "Greek and Latin root words." You will find some nice explanations and a great starting list. By becoming more familiar with root words, an aspiring learner can soon develop great skills for deciphering word meanings, even without a dictionary. In the word "exploration," the root "plor" means to explore. I have included a short list of root words to get you started. Commit these and others you encounter to memory. Begin paying attention to new vocabulary words by noticing the root, the main part of the words.

Root	Meaning	Root	Meaning
astro	stars	geo	earth
audi	hear	micro	small
bene	good	ped	foot
cent	one hundred	poly	many

Bridging the Gap – Suffixes

Suffixes make up the portion of the word often location at the end. In similar manner, search the internet for "free list of common suffixes."

---

[7] (LoveToKnow 2022)

These lists get updated periodically, so selecting a current one to study with will serve you best. In the word "exploration," the suffix -tion or even -ation relates to a process. Putting it all together, exploration means to go "out" + "explore" + "perform a process." Exploration is the process of going out and exploring. Some suffixes change the meaning of the word, while others change the form of it. I have included a small list to get you started. Again, studying these word parts can speed up developing a stronger comfort with vocabulary, reading, and writing.

Suffix	Result	Suffix	Result
-able -ible	Adds "can be done" to meaning	-ies	Plural noun
-ed	Past tense verb	-ing	Verb continuing action
-er -or	Noun, often a person, performing action (ex singer)	-less	Adds "without" to the meaning of the word
-est	Comparative, (extreme – like least or most)	-ly	Transforms an adjective to an adverb
-ful	Adds "full of" to meaning of word	-s, -es	Plural noun

While the English language has many prefixes, roots, and suffixes, by selecting some common lists to memorize and learn will provide a great foundation and help bridge gaps in your vocabulary development. Before proceeding to the next chapter, take time to record some notes from this one into your journal. These notes will prove helpful in your writing and learning journey.

Journal Entry – (Today's Date) Word Parts

After recording your thoughts, make sure to set yourself some goals for practicing and becoming comfortable with the things presented in this chapter. Travel on to the next to learn tips for adding to your word skills.

Summary

Gaining skills in phonics along with the ability to decipher words will help you become more competent as a reader and a writer. Remember to personally challenge yourself to grow in both your strong and weak areas. By facing weak zones, you will build confidence and bridge learning gaps. Spending time to further develop your strengths will help you soar!

Chapter Questions

1. Amy has felt embarrassed about the problem she has sometimes with words that have a "c" or an "s" in them. As a result, she often has difficulty pronouncing many of these words. As Amy's friend, what do you recommend and why?

2. How does developing an understanding of phonics help students improve their spelling abilities?

3. How do you figure out the number of syllables in a vocabulary word?

4. How could dissecting a word into its syllables help improve understanding?

5. How does studying prefixes, roots, and suffixes help students?

Your choice of words makes a huge difference. Afterall, "an elegant monarch butterfly soaring gracefully" does sound more divine than "a butterfly flies."

Chapter 12 Vocabulary Development

Chapter Objectives

- Examine ways to improve vocabulary and increase reading comprehension.

- Explore ways to strengthen the use of new words in your writing.

- Discover how to challenge yourself to write better by adding time and scoring writing games to your activities.

- Learn how to cultivate a joy for writing.

Moving beyond and examining the syllables of words and exploring prefixes, roots, and suffixes, building your vocabulary base will require discipline, diligence, and some amount of strategy. In this chapter, I share some ideas on how to purposefully add more words to your comfort bank.

Vocabulary Building Through Reading Exploration

In this activity, we will explore a way for developing and growing your vocabulary. The students I work with all seem to tolerate and many even enjoy this approach. Additionally, many students who struggle with reading comprehension discover that the main reason for such weakness stems from having a weak vocabulary. By embracing the challenge to improve your vocabulary, you also should see an improvement in reading, writing, and public speaking.

Round #1 The Hunt (10 minutes)

Pick up your textbook or reading material and turn to the next chapter or section. For this round, you will not actually read anything. You will scan the pages with your eyes and look for words. Look for three kinds of words: new, unfamiliar, and cool.

✓ Words that you do not know the meaning or definition,

✓ Words that you have seen before, but do not use very often, and

✓ Words that you think make for cool writing words.

When the timer begins you will scan with your eyes, find the words, and write them down in your journal book. Aim to find at least 25 words during this round. You may even want to group or sort them by the word types: new, unfamiliar, and cool. Create a new journal entry for this exercise.

Journal Entry – (Today's Date) Capturing words from (Your Book)

If the timer goes off before you have found at least twenty-five words, keep looking. Remind yourself that you will scan, not read during this round. I have observed that students who do struggle with the word search exercise do so because they read instead of scanning. Did you know that your eyes and brain connect in ways we do not fully understand? Simply move your eyes across the page and let the brain enjoy finding the words.

Round #2 Meaning

Do you know what each word means? Take time to look up new and unfamiliar words. Once you find the definitions, feel free to write notes to help you remember these words. As you interact with the new words, make yourself comfortable and get ready to use them in writing.

Round #3 Use it!

This next round can vary widely depending on skill and grade level. Also, this third round has two main variations or three ways to play. We will try them all, so you can get a feel for each. Use your journal book to record the two methods.

Special Note: Round #3 works best if paired with someone else. However, if playing the game solo, you can challenge yourself to outscore prior rounds. Beat your record!

Variation A

You will have ten minutes. Get the timer ready. You will look at the list of words written earlier and try to write just **one sentence**. Each of the words from the list will earn you one point when placed into the sentence. At the end of the ten minutes, one **sentence** should contain many of the words from your list. Be careful to correctly punctuate!

Variation B

You will have ten minutes. Get the timer ready. Look at the list of words written earlier and write one story. You may use as many sentences as needed. Each word from the list included in your story will earn you one point. At the end of the ten minutes, the one story should contain many of the words from your list.

Note: This game does have a competitive feel and can be played simultaneously with different people. Players will benefit by learning more words from each other.

Variation C – Group Word Raid

Each person may have a varying number of words. So, to even out the playing field and add a sharing component, variation C includes a "word raid" or a voluntary exchange. If a player found more than 25 words, then he or she could choose a word to cheerfully give another player. Thoughtfully consider the words to give away. The player receiving the new word would need to look up the definition as needed.

Mystery Word Raid - Like card games, each player numbers their wordlist. Other players may then request a mystery word, "Give me word number 4." Take turns swapping mystery words.

One Sentence or Short Story – Together, players decide if they will write just one sentence or a short story. Each player will normally have the same number of words for this game. Then, set the timer for ten minutes. Use as many of the words on the list in your writing.

Round #4 Scoring

When the timer goes off, signaling the end of the round, use a highlighter or somehow identify each of the words used in your writing. Count the marked words. Each of these count as one point. Yes, you may use the same word twice and earn two points. However, the second usage of the word may not reside in the same or adjacent sentence as the one containing the first appearance. (Maximum of two points per word) Tally up your points.

Special note: Players may challenge how opponents use words in sentences. If everyone agrees that a word has been improperly included in a sentence, then the player in violation of grammar or word meaning usage must deduct one point.

Share

Go around the circle and take turns. "I earned ___ points." After sharing the number of points earned, take turns reading what you wrote. The player with the most points wins the round.

Increase skill level and create a more competitive feel by doing this activity multiple times. Each time choose a different chapter or section in the reading material to pull words. ("Let's go for the highest three out of five!")

Jazzy Words and the Thesaurus

Your choice of words makes a huge difference. Afterall, "an elegant monarch butterfly gracefully soars" does sound more divine than "a butterfly flies." In this next exercise, look at that last story you wrote, or flip through your journal, and find a recently written one. Open your favorite thesaurus, and practice trading out plain sounding words. Also, consider adding adjectives and adverbs. Adjectives will mostly help dress up nouns, while adverbs get paired with verbs. (Rewrite your story to allow for ample space or copy and paste prior to editing if using a digital device.) This will allow you to track the progression and see progress.

Make the following adjustments:

- ✓ Trade out plain words for new ones found in the thesaurus.
- ✓ Add adjectives.
- ✓ Add adverbs.

Create this new version in the next journal entry!

Journal Entry – (Today's Date) – Name of your story

Writers often spend hours assessing just the right words to use to intently engage their readers. Some people share such expertise in blogs, website articles, and misc. postings online. Quite routinely, when I need some ideas for describing story scenes, or even key characters, browsing the internet provides me with a rich wealth of writing insight.

Building word power skills would not feel complete without including the writing community. The adage "Don't reinvent the wheel" could apply to writing. May I suggest thinking of key words to describe a scene in a story, then type those key words into the search bar of your web browser. Before clicking "search" or pressing enter/return, add the words "writing words for" to the front of these key words. For example, if your story has an ocean scene, consider going to a web browser and searching for "writing words for ocean." The browser will display various links to explore that may prove helpful. Test it out! Look at the last story you wrote or flip through your journal to find one. Assess the setting for the story and come up with one or two key words to describe it. Next, go to the web browser and search for "writing words for," and include your key words. Explore some of the links presented. Do you have any new ideas? Take time to experiment and write another version of your story.

Journal Entry – (Today's Date) – Your Story's Title

Vocabulary building happens as you continue diligently working with words. Sensory descriptive writing pulls the readers in because they feel like you have brought them along. Continue practicing by adding new words to your vocabulary. Explore other tools such as www.vocabulary.com to further refine the art.[8] Do you see improvement in your writing? How will developing your word power help you? Take some time to journal your thoughts.

Journal Entry – (Today's Date) – The Benefits of Word Power

Summary

Clearly, having a strong vocabulary and using the techniques and tools mentioned in this chapter will enhance your writing (and improve reading comprehension). As this happens, writing becomes even more enjoyable for you and for your readers! Take time to set personal goals. Set aside hours to purposefully work on increasing your comfort level with new vocabulary.

---

[8] (Vocabulary.com, a Division of IXL Learning 2022)

Chapter Questions

1. How can identifying new words in reading materials help to improve your reading comprehension?

2. In this chapter, you searched for three types of words: new, unfamiliar, and cool. How does this process turn into a useful method for improving your writing?

3. Did adding the timed game make the process more enjoyable? Explain.

4. Will you challenge yourself to repeat this process in the future? Explain your plans and the results you hope to see.

Section 6: Essays and Reports

Entire books written on the art of writing essays and reports sit on library shelves around the world. In this section, I do not intend to cover every aspect of this subject. Rather, I believe you will benefit more from a more simplified approach, one that seeks to demystify and present the writing of essays and reports in an easier to understand manner. I find that once students grasp some basic techniques, they no longer shy away from school assignments that require turning in papers. Additionally, following certain standards or protocols should not weigh a student down to the point of hindering free flowing expression. Like David disrobing the king's bulky armor in his quest to stand up for the Israelites and fight the giant Goliath, this section will attempt to encourage you to express yourself in writing without feeling so weighed down by heavy rules. I have included an introduction to standards for us to visit after solidifying writing basics. You will have a great foundation for writing three main types of essays: opinion, argumentative, and informational. Additionally, we will step beyond the standard five to six paragraph essay structure and explore report writing.

Much like snagging a fish, a hook serves to grab the attention of readers, perhaps ones perusing through several different titles. Will the reader read past the first sentence?

Chapter 13 Essay Writing

Chapter Objectives

- Explore and identify the five elements for forming an essay's introduction paragraph.

- Define the term hook and discover how to attract readers.

- Understand the importance of a thesis statement and practice creating one.

- Distinguish between opinion, argumentative, and informational (expository) writing.

- Discover how transition sentences impact the overall flow of the essay.

- Construct body paragraphs that clarify and expound upon the thesis statement.

- Identify the importance of adding a call to action to the essay's conclusion.

In this chapter, we will consider two types of essays, opinion and argumentative. You have most likely already begun writing essays. However, as we discuss essay writing and you work through the exercises, challenge yourself to strive for excellence. This discussion will

167

benefit beginner and advanced essay writers. Start by selecting a topic to write about, then proceed with your journal book in hand.

Introduction Paragraph

The introductory paragraph houses the foundation, the part that everything else sits upon. Much like building a house, this foundation must have a solid layout and meaningful content to hold up the weight of the rest of the essay. Writers and educators offer various recommendations and ideas regarding the overall structure of the introduction. We will start out with the following setup:

- ✓ Hook
- ✓ Context or Background
- ✓ Prompt or Question Being Asked
- ✓ Thesis Statement
- ✓ Transition or Invitation Sentence

We will briefly discuss these elements one by one.

The Hook

Treat yourself to some richly fascinating tourism

without having to travel far.

I hope people will stop and read my essay about vacationing close to home. Much like snagging a fish, a hook serves to grab the attention of readers, perhaps ones perusing through several different titles. Will the reader read past the first sentence? Creating a great hook sentence will increase the likelihood of sparking enough curiosity that someone will decide to read more of the essay. A hook can consist of a catchy quote, a provoking question, an interesting statistic or fact, a figurative appealing sentence, or other attention getting thoughts.

Velasco 1

Nancy B. Velasco

Professor JK Peabody

English 101 Intro to Writing

5 December 20--

Vacationing Close to Home

Treat yourself to some richly fascinating tourism without having to travel far. City dwellers often enjoy escaping the bustle of it all and traveling to exotic places abroad. Those living in rural parts, desiring to interact with more people, eagerly hop on a plane and travel to populated areas full of activities and sights. Minimalists seek a simpler more affordable vacation spot nearby to just relax. Would a vacation along the coast of California or one across the ocean best appeal to individuals needing to get away? Visitors prefer to tour the coast of California because it has beautiful butterflies, sparkling ocean fronts, and lovely artwork. Read on to discover how to embark on such a relaxing vacation without having to cross the ocean.

Think about your topic now. Begin a new journal entry and brainstorm ideas for catching someone's attention. You may need to draft a few versions before choosing a hook.

Journal Entry – (Today's Date) Hook Practice

After drafting the hook, make sure to read it out loud, and ask yourself, "Would I stop to read the rest?" Once you have a nice hook, clue the reader as to how your topic came about.

Context or Background

After catching the attention of the reader, much like an announcer or emcee at a celebration, the writer will share why this essay's topic has risen enough in importance to even write about it. To effectively layout the context, ask yourself two questions:

- ✓ Who shows interest in this topic or issue?

- ✓ Why are they interested in it?

I recommend introducing your topic using a neutral tone. Avoid unveiling how you personally feel about an issue until presenting the thesis statement. Much like a referee, briefly present the overriding beliefs held by two opposing sides or viewpoints.

Vacationing Close to Home

Treat yourself to some richly fascinating tourism without having to travel far. City dwellers often enjoy escaping the bustle of it all and traveling to exotic places abroad. Those living in rural parts, desiring to interact with more people, eagerly hop on a plane and travel to populated areas full of activities and sights. Minimalists seek a simpler more affordable vacation spot nearby to just relax. Would a vacation along the coast of California or one across the ocean

---

Look at the topic you selected. Can you think of two opposite views or perspectives coming from two groups of people? What do these two groups believe about your topic? In your journal, write two to four sentences to capture the overall beliefs of these two opposite views.

Journal Entry – (Today's Date) Context/Background

Read what you wrote carefully. Make sure you do not have any sentence fragments. Also, verify that you have written the main belief of each of the opposing sides. Especially, double check that the reader would not yet know which side you personally lean towards.

If your essay falls under the "opinion writing" category instead of the "argumentative" one, then presenting both sides in the introduction though not mandatory, does help the reader understand your thoughts on who might find this topic of interest. After solidifying the context for your essay, pop the question.

Prompt or Question

The question, or writing prompt being addressed, appears next. Notice the placement. It goes after the context or background and just prior to the thesis statement. Have you ever read something that just went on and on endlessly without even knowing what the writer meant?

---

dwellers often enjoy escaping the bustle of it all and traveling to exotic places abroad. Those living in rural parts, desiring to interact with more people, eagerly hop on a plane and travel to populated areas full of activities and sights. Minimalists seek a simpler more affordable vacation spot nearby to just relax. Would a vacation along the coast of California or one across the ocean best appeal to individuals needing to get away? Visitors prefer to tour the coast of California because it has beautiful butterflies, sparkling ocean fronts, and lovely artwork. Read on to

---

Picture arriving late to a get together with friends. Everyone has pulled up comfortable chairs, sat down, and commenced talking prior to your arrival. A cordial hostess would politely catch you up on the conversation, provide some refreshments, and invite you to join the others. If instead of letting you know the jest of the conversation, the hostess just left you to fend for yourself, awkwardly, after finding a seat, minutes may tick by before the actual topic becomes apparent.

Similarly, failure to include the question up for discussion leaves the reader in the dark, with no sense of the writing context. The hook, the context, and question set the stage for communicating your thoughts and beliefs.

Take a few minutes and practice wording the prompt or question sentence. Given the placement, in between the context or background and the thesis statement, you will want to be careful of redundancy. Read what you write out loud, if some words get repeated, then consider using a thesaurus and finding other words to express the same idea. Having the same wording multiple times could come across as an insult to the intelligence of your readers. Keep it fresh and unique! Travel on to the most important sentence of all!

Thesis statement

In the thesis statement, you share your perspectives and views with the readers. Keep the following in mind when preparing the thesis statement.

The thesis statement does not unravel everything. Briefly answer the question being asked. I encourage students to think of three reasons or three points about this topic. These three points will unfold more in the body paragraphs, so for now, simply list them. Try to word the thesis statement so that it does not sound too repetitious.

> Treat yourself to some richly fascinating tourism without having to travel far. City dwellers often enjoy escaping the bustle of it all and traveling to exotic places abroad. Those living in rural parts, desiring to interact with more people, eagerly hop on a plane and travel to populated areas full of activities and sights. Minimalists seek a simpler more affordable vacation spot nearby to just relax. Would a vacation along the coast of California or one across the ocean best appeal to individuals needing to get away? Visitors prefer to tour the coast of California because it has beautiful butterflies, sparkling ocean fronts, and lovely artwork. Read on to discover how to embark on such a relaxing vacation without having to cross the ocean.

Create a new journal entry to practice developing a thesis for your topic.

Journal Entry – (Today's Date) Thesis

Read out loud and listen carefully. Do the sentences written so far make sense? Do they flow nicely with a unique voice? If so, pen the transition or invitation sentence.

Transition/Invitation Sentence

Finally, conclude the introduction by politely welcoming the reader to continue. This welcoming sentence serves as a transition that takes the reader from the introduction to the body portion of the essay.

While I personally like to include such a transition, some teachers do instruct their classes to omit it. Though such instruction does not align with mine, I will most likely not grade your work. So, follow the

directions set forth by your teacher or professor.

Journal Entry – (Today's Date) Invitation/Transition

I recommend keeping the invite brief and to the point. "This topic

deserves further attention." -- Or – "This critical issue warrants further

discussion." Practice drafting out a succinct welcoming. Then, take time

to read what you have put together so far. You should have the

complete introduction now.

Body Paragraphs

In the thesis statement, you included three main considerations.

These three things unfold in the three body paragraphs – one paragraph

each. Though the content varies depending on the topic and type of

essay, in essence, you will take each of the considerations one by one

and break them down further.

For example, my thesis statement may look like the following:

Visitors prefer to tour the coast of California because it

has beautiful butterflies, sparkling ocean fronts, and lovely

artwork.

In preparing three body paragraphs to further explain the above thesis statement, notice the three main items: beautiful butterflies, sparkling ocean fronts, and lovely artwork. Each of these would set the stage for a body paragraph. Can I find enough information about the butterflies along the coast? Ideally, sharing three key things about such butterflies would make for a solid first body paragraph.

Thinking about my own experience in seeking out the butterflies, understanding the migration path and season would prove helpful to the readers. Adding references and making mention of tools for following the path would add integrity to the paper. Additionally, explaining that certain greenery attracts these winged creatures might help the reader more successfully locate some specimens. I could additionally lead the readers to picture files showing what these trees look like. Finally, after scratching my head trying to come up with a third thought, browsing the internet proved helpful. I learned about Pacific Grove experiencing changes in the number of monarch butterflies migrating to the area. Destruction to the habitat saw the number of monarchs decrease; however, thankfully, in 2022 the number went back up. The rough experience in 2020 left some debating on declaring the butterfly an endangered species.

No matter which details I select for my butterfly paragraph, the topic sentence should help the reader by providing directions:

To fully appreciate the butterflies, consider migration paths, plant life that attracts the monarchs, and annual fluctuations in the species population.

Structurally, the body paragraph might include a sequence such as this one:

- ✓ Topic sentence
- ✓ First main observation sentence and explanation of source backing it up.
- ✓ Second main observation sentence and explanation of source backing it up.
- ✓ Third main observation sentence and explanation of source backing it up.
- ✓ Transition sentence (Consider mentioning the butterflies and the sparkling ocean fronts in the same sentence.)

Body Paragraph 1

To fully appreciate the butterflies, consider migration paths, plant life that attracts the monarchs, and annual fluctuations in the species population. Pack a suitcase and follow the butterflies along California's coast October through February. Pacific Grove, California provides interesting sightseeing and even hosts a museum for educating people about butterflies. According to the Pacific Grove website, monarchs travel each year when butterfly eggs get laid, these get imprinted with special genetic coding, mysteriously enabling a new generation to find its way back. Despite the beauty of it all, and this Butterfly City's ordinance to fine those molesting the monarchs, unfortunately, in 2020, the researchers and volunteers noticed a delay in the arrival of these beauties (Ogasa). Additionally, the monarchs did not arrive in as large numbers as in prior years. Monterey Herald shares that after careful study, the scientists

Velasco 2

hypothesize that parasite ridden milkweeds may have contributed to the decline. Parasites can inadvertently kill off the eggs. Thankfully, the numbers have once again increased for 2022 (Associated Press). Travelers to Pacific Grove might want to bring some binoculars and look up high. According to the city's website, "Arriving in October, monarch butterflies cluster together on pine, cypress and eucalyptus trees in the Sanctuary" (Monarch Sanctuary). While checking out the butterfly landings, tourists also enjoy the sparkling ocean shoreline rest stops.

I am saving the URLs (links) that provided the information for my body paragraph. These will prove necessary in a later step. We want to give credit to each of the writers for such information. Failure to do so results in plagiarism. We will return to explore and discuss intext citations and reference page entries shortly.

Before moving on to the essay summary paragraph, build out all three body paragraphs. Notice something! Initially, my personal knowledge of butterflies would not have been enough to write a solid body paragraph. Searching and browsing the internet uncovered important details. I imagined traveling as a tourist and asked myself questions along the way. Additionally, the sequencing and connectivity of the sentences sprung from the topic sentence. The last sentence serves to connect body paragraph one to body paragraph two. It mentions butterflies and ocean shorelines.

You can test out developing a body paragraph. Look at the thesis sentence constructed for your topic. Create your first body paragraph to support the first important point. Make sure to save URL links.

Journal Entry – (Today's Date) Body Paragraph 1

Proofread your work, then follow along as I share regarding my second body paragraph next.

Body Paragraph #2

In similar fashion, body paragraph two will focus on the ocean shoreline spots that tourists can enjoy. We will want to find three key things about visiting the shoreline spots. After placing these into a topic sentence, we can explore more content to solidify the three considerations noted. Again, supportive references help to strengthen the paper. Writers have their own styles. I prefer to paraphrase the source information and maybe include one or two quotations.

> Monterey's Cannery Row, Carmel by the Sea, and Pebble Beach offer some of the most scenic delights. Certainly, if traveling all the way from city life to visit the Pacific Grove area, Monterey's Cannery Row hosts a great variety of relaxing fun mixed with ocean splashes and sunshine (*Welcome to cannery row*). Cute hotels next to the water, tasty fine dining on seafood, the adventures of kayaking, and sightseeing at the large aquarium will provide a nice family experience. Make sure to bring some money for use at the little shops, especially the candy store! Carmel by the Sea offers places for winding down, relaxing and taking in the splashes of the ocean (Carmel-by-the-Sea). Visitors enjoy dining in the fine restaurants. Carmel also has a very artistic appeal, attracting painters and art enthusiasts. Pebble Beach boasts of its 17-mile scenic drive as it sits along the ocean front (*Golf Resorts, Courses & Spa Vacations*). Its beautiful greenery attracts golfers and everyone who likes a more open fresh air feel during their vacation experience. Relaxing and having fun in these lovely coastal towns along the western coast of California would not be complete without considering the artwork.

Again, I will save the source URLs associated with body paragraph two. These will become necessary for noting references. Remember to include a transition sentence linking body paragraphs 2 and 3 together.

Body Paragraph #3

The building of body paragraph three will flow in a similar manner. By this time, as a writer, you will most likely have a great desire to visit the area of Pacific Grove. At least, I do!

> Stop by the Monterey area and take in the beautiful paintings of Thomas Kinkade, the writing nostalgia of John Steinbeck, and enjoy symphonies and jazz bands. Thomas Kinkade elegantly captures a sparkle of light in each of his thoughtful and popular paintings. While Thomas Kinkade galleries exist in other parts of America, the galleries in the Monterey area hold

> the positions closest to the scenes captured (*Paintings of Monterey and Carmel*). Additionally, these served as the actual studios for Mr. Kinkade. Tourists may even get the opportunity to meet him or his protégés and watch them paint. John Steinbeck lived in the Pacific Grove area, and people now enjoy touring some of his homes. One site advertises renting the studio as a place to lay one's head (*John Steinbeck's writer's studio: Home of classic American author (30 Night Min) - pacific grove*). That might prove a nice touch to share with friends of having slept

Again, I am saving the source URLs that go with body paragraph three. As you can see, the internet often provides an abundance of information. As the writer, you will want to carefully locate the best sources to include in your essay.

181

in Steinbeck's studio. Visit the stomping grounds of Steinbeck (*Steinbeck's Asilomar Sample Itineraries: Asilomar conference grounds: Pacific grove ca*). Touring the National Steinbeck Museum also would nicely round out an art visit. For more of an evening out type of art appreciation, visit the Monterey Symphony (Monterey Symphony). Then, take part in the jazz festival (Monterey Jazz Festival 65 - September 23-25, 20--). The jazz festival has already concluded for this year; however, check back in 20--. Both popular locations offer an evening of musical relaxation. Make sure to check the calendar for the upcoming performances and book tickets. Before heading out of the Pacific Grove area, while checking out butterflies, make sure to stop in at the Pacific Grove Public Library and check out Book Grove books (Pacific Grove Books). Special books showcase local writers and their published works. These would provide more descriptive narratives about visiting and traveling in the area. Taking in the fine arts of painting, writing, and music adds a very warm and appealing touch to the vacation package.

The Conclusion or Summary

The last paragraph will nicely remind readers of the thesis statement but use different wording. You will want to share your main rationale for writing the essay. Lessen repetition so as not to insult your audience. They have already read the first version of your thesis statement.

Next, good writers will include closing remarks. Much like conversing with professionals about something important, closing remarks emphasize one key thought that the writer personally finds most compelling.

Clearly, scheduling some time to travel along the coast, seeing the delightful butterflies, staying over at some beautiful scenic hotels along the way, enjoying arts and music, and visiting the places of famous writers and painters does sound like a very appealing and affordable vacation. After living in the area for so many years, residents can vacation in style as local

tourists. Individuals and families will save money by traveling within the state and having fun. Consider planning out such a beautiful vacation today and come back relaxed!

Works Cited

Finally, state a call to action. Consider the audience who will read this essay. What steps could they take next? This step should line up with your thesis statement. If the essay expresses ideas for traveling along the western coast of California, then the call to action may encourage the reader to check in at a particular hotel in the area and schedule the trip today. If the writing sought to persuade parents to urge school leaders to have stricter policies regarding social distancing, then the call to action may encourage them to call or write the district office. The summary should contain these three elements: a restatement of the thesis, some closing remarks, and a call to action.

Transitions Paragraph to Paragraph

After drafting out the five paragraphs, you will want to go through and add transitional words or phrases. Particularly, sentence flow transitions and paragraph to paragraph ones will prove helpful. Sentence flow transitions consist of the small words or phrases at the beginning of the sentences that create a smoother feel upon reading the paragraph. Build upon this sentence-to-sentence flow by stepping back and looking at the paragraph level overall.

Another way to improve the flow has to do with sentence structure. Make sure each paragraph includes a nice mixture of simple, complex, and compound sentences. Read each paragraph out loud and modify sentences until they sound smooth.

Practice, Practice, Practice

Writing a basic five paragraph essay does take practice. If you struggle to write the perfect essay, go back through the steps presented in this chapter. Pick different topics to write about. Repeat the writing process until you feel comfortable. You will need to practice often.

If you decide to turn the essay into an argumentative one, then add a fourth body paragraph. Your topic sentence will indicate the main opposing argument and briefly defend your position. "While many tourists enjoy traveling to the mountains, the beautiful spots along the coast provide for a better getaway." You would strongly proceed but briefly explain why your choice trumps the other. "Instead of harsh mountain trail hiking, the entire family can relax by the ocean. Vacationers find roaming in the outdoors, taking in the spacious ocean views, admiring artwork in galleries, plus chasing the amazing butterflies provides a more enjoyable experience. Besides, who wants to get stuck in a mountain cabin?"

Summary

Most students encounter the five-paragraph essay. As noted in the prior discussion, connecting thoughts together lies at the heart or the foundation of essay writing. Much like building a house, the introduction provides strong support for holding up the body. Like catching a basketball or football, then tossing it to team players, the thesis statement briefly announces what the body paragraphs will contain. The transition or invitation sentence takes a turn and tosses the flow to the first body paragraph. After the last body paragraph, the summary goes in for the closing wrap up by reminding the reader of the main points and encouraging further action.

Continue to the next chapter and see how the principle of connectivity weaves itself through other types of writing. For example, we will look at the process of creating reports. Most classes, and even businesses, will require you to submit reports.

Chapter Questions

1. Considering the five elements of an introduction paragraph, create an introduction in response to the prompt, "Should gasoline sellers be required to set their prices the same regardless of their location?"

2. Define the term **hook**. Give an example of a good one.

3. Define **context/background**. Thoughtful pondering: Why do you think writers choose to remain neutral when writing this portion of the introduction. Why do they wait until the thesis statement to disclose their views on the matter?

4. Look again at question 1. Challenge yourself by adding body paragraphs to your essay.

5. How can you develop a better flow in your essay? Read your body paragraphs out loud. What can you change to help create a nice flow?

6. Define **call to action**. Can you think of why an essay may come across weaker if the writer failed to include a call to action?

7. Next, add the summary or conclusion to your essay, making sure to include a call to action.

8. When would you use an argumentative essay instead of an opinion one?

Nancy B. Velasco

Professor JK Peabody

English 101 Intro to Writing

5 December 20--

Vacationing Close to Home

Treat yourself to some richly fascinating tourism without having to travel far. City dwellers often enjoy escaping the bustle of it all and traveling to exotic places abroad. Those living in rural parts, desiring to interact with more people, eagerly hop on a plane and travel to populated areas full of activities and sights. Minimalists seek a simpler more affordable vacation spot nearby to just relax. Would a vacation along the coast of California or one across the ocean best appeal to individuals needing to get away? Visitors prefer to tour the coast of California because it has beautiful butterflies, sparkling ocean fronts, and lovely artwork. Read on to discover how to embark on such a relaxing vacation without having to cross the ocean.

To fully appreciate the butterflies, consider migration paths, plant life that attracts the monarchs, and annual fluctuations in the species population. Pack a suitcase and follow the butterflies along California's coast October through February. Pacific Grove, California provides interesting sightseeing and even hosts a museum for educating people about butterflies. According to the Pacific Grove website, monarchs travel each year when butterfly eggs get laid, these get imprinted with special genetic coding, mysteriously enabling a new generation to find its way back. Despite the beauty of it all, and this Butterfly City's ordinance to fine those molesting the monarchs, unfortunately, in 2020, the researchers and volunteers noticed a delay in the arrival of these beauties (Ogasa). Additionally, the monarchs did not arrive in as large numbers as in prior years. Monterey Herald shares that after careful study, the scientists hypothesize that parasite ridden milkweeds may have contributed to the decline. Parasites can inadvertently kill off the eggs. Thankfully, the numbers have once again increased for 2022 (Associated Press). Travelers to Pacific Grove might want to bring some binoculars and look up high. According to the city's website, "Arriving in October, monarch butterflies cluster together on pine, cypress and eucalyptus trees in the Sanctuary" (Monarch Sanctuary). While checking out the butterfly landings, tourists also enjoy the sparkling ocean shoreline rest stops.

Monterey's Cannery Row, Carmel by the Sea, and Pebble Beach offer some of the most scenic delights. Certainly, if traveling all the way from city life to visit the Pacific Grove area, Monterey's Cannery Row hosts a great variety of relaxing fun mixed with ocean splashes and sunshine (*Welcome to cannery row*). Cute hotels next to the water, tasty fine dining on seafood, the adventures of kayaking, and sightseeing at the large aquarium will provide a nice family experience. Make sure to bring some money for use at the little shops, especially the candy store! Carmel by the Sea offers places for winding down, relaxing and taking in the splashes of the ocean (Carmel-by-the-Sea). Visitors enjoy dining in the fine restaurants. Carmel also has a very artistic appeal, attracting painters and art enthusiasts. Pebble Beach boasts of its 17-mile scenic drive as it sits along the ocean front (*Golf Resorts, Courses & Spa Vacations*). Its beautiful greenery attracts golfers and everyone who likes a more open fresh air feel during their vacation experience. Relaxing and having fun in these lovely coastal towns along the western coast of California would not be complete without considering the artwork.

Stop by the Monterey area and take in the beautiful paintings of Thomas Kinkade, the writing nostalgia of John Steinbeck, and enjoy symphonies and jazz bands. Thomas Kinkade elegantly captures a sparkle of light in each of his thoughtful and popular paintings. While Thomas Kinkade galleries exist in other parts of America, the galleries in the Monterey area hold the positions closest to the scenes captured (*Paintings of Monterey and Carmel*). Additionally, these served as the actual studios for Mr. Kinkade. Tourists may even get the opportunity to meet him or his protégés and watch them paint. John Steinbeck lived in the Pacific Grove area, and people now enjoy touring some of his homes. One site advertises renting the studio as a place to lay one's head (*John Steinbeck's writer's studio: Home of classic American author (30 Night Min) - pacific grove*). That might prove a nice touch to share with friends of having slept in Steinbeck's studio. Visit the stomping grounds of Steinbeck (*Steinbeck's Asilomar Sample Itineraries: Asilomar conference grounds: Pacific grove ca*). Touring the National Steinbeck Museum also would nicely round out an art visit. For more of an evening out type of art appreciation, visit the Monterey Symphony (Monterey Symphony). Then, take part in the jazz festival (Monterey Jazz Festival 65 - September 23-25, 20--). The jazz festival has already concluded for this year; however, check back in 20--. Both popular locations offer an evening of musical relaxation. Make sure to check the calendar for the upcoming performances and book tickets. Before heading out of the Pacific Grove area, while checking out butterflies, make sure to stop in at the Pacific Grove Public Library and check out Book Grove books (Pacific Grove Books). Special books showcase local writers and their published works. These would provide more descriptive narratives about visiting and traveling in the area. Taking in the fine arts of painting, writing, and music adds a very warm and appealing touch to the vacation package.

Clearly, scheduling some time to travel along the coast, seeing the delightful butterflies, staying over at some beautiful scenic hotels along the way, enjoying arts and music, and visiting the places of famous writers and painters does sound like a very appealing and affordable vacation. After living in the area for so many years, residents can vacation in style as local tourists. Individuals and families will save money by traveling within the state and having fun. Consider planning out such a beautiful vacation today and come back relaxed!

Works Cited

Associated Press. "After Record Low, Monarch Butterflies Return to California." NBCNews.com, NBCUniversal News Group, 20 Nov. 2021, https://www.nbcnews.com/science/environment/record-low-monarch-butterflies-return-california-rcna5845.

Carmel-by-the-Sea, California. "By-the-Sea, California Official Travel Site." Visit Carmel By-the-Sea, Carmel By the Sea, California, https://www.carmelcalifornia.com/.

"Golf Resorts, Courses & Spa Vacations." Pebble Beach Resorts, Pebble Beach Company, Nov. 2022, https://www.pebblebeach.com/.

"John Steinbeck's Writer's Studio: Home of Classic American Author (30 Night Min) - Pacific Grove." Vrbo, Vrbo, an Expedia Group Company, 2022, https://www.vrbo.com/485366?noDates=true&unitId=1068547.

McNair, Josh. "John Steinbeck's Museum & House in Salinas." California Through My Lens, California Through My Lens, 27 Oct. 2021, https://californiathroughmylens.com/national-stienbeck-center/.

"Monarch Sanctuary." City of Pacific Grove, Pacific Grove, CA, 2022, https://www.cityofpacificgrove.org/our_city/departments/public_works/city_owned_infrastructure/buildings___grounds/monarch_sanctuary.php. Accessed 5 Dec. 2022.

"Monterey Jazz Festival 65 - September 23-25, 2022." 65th Annual Monterey Jazz Festival, 26
    Sept. 2022, https://montereyjazzfestival.org/.

Monterey Symphony. Monterey Symphony, Monterey Symphony, 2022,
    https://www.montereysymphony.org/.

Ogasa, Nikk. "Butterfly Town: Trying to Find the Missing Monarchs." *Monterey Herald*,
    MediaNews Group, 23 Nov. 2020, https://www.montereyherald.com/2020/11/22/butterfly-
    town-trying-to-find-the-missing-monarchs/.

Pacific Grove Books. "Life in Pacific Grove, Books That Inform, Entertain, and Enlighten." Life
    in Pacific Grove, Pacific Grove Books, 2019, https://lifeinpacificgrove.com/.

"Paintings of Monterey and Carmel." Thomas Kinkade Carmel Monterey Placerville, The
    Thomas Kinkade Company, 2019, https://thomaskinkadeca.com/paintings-of-monterey-
    and-carmel/.

"Steinbeck's Asilomar Sample Itineraries: Asilomar Conference Grounds: Pacific Grove Ca."
    Asilomar, Aramark 2022 Asilomar Conference Grounds, 2022,
    https://www.visitasilomar.com/things-to-do/sample-itineraries/steinbecks-asilomar/.

"Welcome to Cannery Row." *Cannery Row, Monterrey, California*, Cannery Row, 17 Mar.
    2021, https://canneryrow.com/.

Continue unloading your

thoughts until nothing else

mentally emerges from your mind.

You will want to then look for new

ideas.

Chapter 14 Report Writing

Chapter Objectives

- Discover how researchers often begin. Despite having a limited understanding of the problem in question, they dive in with excellence.

- Explore the benefits of brain dumps and brainstorming.

- Identify best practices for developing a cohesive team while brainstorming.

- Discuss the importance of conducting a literature review.

- Consider the use of search engine tools and their power in assisting with gathering resources.

- Practice zooming in to define a report's focus.

- Develop a system for organizing useful materials.

Come along now as we examine how to go from a basic five paragraph essay to writing reports. As we begin, think about structure, sequencing, and connections. Observe that the best reports entail at least some level of research. In this chapter, we will look closely at subject matter expertise, research methods, gathering data, and organizing thoughts. While reports vary in terms of content and structure, some common threads weave consistently through scholarly and business style reports.

Expertise

Writing in primary or elementary school does not normally require an expert level of understanding. Afterall, third graders have not necessarily studied the ins and outs of subjects such as chemistry, biology, social studies, or even earth science. As students advance in academia, teachers, professors, and the pupils themselves expect a higher level of competency. The writing exercises given in such classes seek to extract comprehension and insight. In creating reports, students will communicate at higher levels of critical thinking and innovation.

The Brain Dump

Scholarly students must commence by assessing their initial understanding regarding the subject of focus. I like to call this my "brain dump stage." At this point in the process, as a scholar, you will want to capture the unloading of mental thoughts about a subject matter. How you personally conduct a brain dump might prove different from my style. Brain dumps fit the person, not the other way around. Some people like to write full sentences at this point. Others prefer to create an outline. Some folks take index cards and make separate categories or points on each one. I tend to gravitate towards using thought maps.

So, the process kicks off with you asking yourself, "What do I already know about this topic? What do I believe? What opinions, facts, or insights have I already acquired up to this point in time?" In my case, the middle of the page often serves as the spot for recording the main core question or topic. Each separate consideration surrounding this main topic becomes a branch of the thought map tree. Smaller details underneath these elements further extend out from the branches. As shared in my earlier writing on note taking, depending on the complexity of the subject in question, multiple-colored pens or pencils might prove helpful and even make the process more interesting.

Continue unloading your thoughts until nothing else mentally emerges from your mind. Afterwards, you will proceed to search for new ideas. Take time now to practice the brain dump exercise. Can you come up with some great ideas for the best way to clean up the community's park? You pick the park to focus on. You create the plans!

Journal Entry – (Today's Date) Park Cleanup Brain dump

Set goals for confirming and finding support for personal beliefs and ideas already recorded. Though many people may respect your gut level opinions, backing these up by finding credible references will add integrity to your report. Further, explore areas less traveled. In my case, the branches that have very little twigs springing off them, indicating my own lack of knowledge, serve as welcome flags for exploration. To gain greater understanding, lean on the expertise of other people, after all, you do not know everything yet. One person, even one expert, does not know everything. Make sure to "hear" the views of multiple individuals.

Brainstorm Sessions

While a brain dump normally involves your own mental pouring out process, a team of people meeting together could prove beneficial. A brainstorming session with a team allows for a wider inclusion of ideas by giving each person an opportunity to share. Ideally each should personally engage in a brain dump prior to the full team gathering for a brainstorming session. However, time elements do play a part in determining the extent of such effort. Therefore, combinations of the brain dump and brainstorming process exist in major corporations today. Standard practice for a team brainstorming session includes three consistent elements:

- Team members share thoughts, and the group's brainstorming initiator will capture the heart of the ideas expressed during the meeting. All attendees should visually see these ideas accumulated on a whiteboard, a digital map, a stand-up flip chart, or other presentation medium.

- The initiator must encourage input and create an environment of acceptance. Attendees must respect each other and yield to the process. Avoid judging, criticizing, or evaluating during this phase. Capture ideas until none remain.

- Periods of silence fill the room as responses decrease. Keep squeezing the sponge. Often the best ideas come next!

Test out have a brainstorming session by getting together with friends or classmates and sharing your ideas about cleaning up the community park. Record your group's insights in the next journal.

Journal Entry – (Today's Date) Park Brainstorming

Literature Review

In a nutshell, literature review means to assess what others have already discovered about this topic. At this juncture, a good researcher will explore different forms of media until satisfied. Media includes journal articles, books, videos, artwork, podcasts, websites, speeches, plays, interviews, news casts, testimonies, and more. Ask the question, "How have people knowledgeable regarding my subject matter communicated ideas and thoughts?" If your teacher or professor assigns a report, get started right away. Waiting until the day before the due date spells disaster. Start early! This literature review step could take minutes, hours, and even days. In the case of a graduate-level thesis, it could even take months. Field researchers often take several years to add to a beginning knowledge base.

Do some literature review research and discover how other people have successfully implemented a community park cleaning or other similar activity. Record your key insights and observations in the following journal.

Journal Entry – (Today's Date) Literature Review Park Cleanup

---

My undergraduate bachelor's degree had an entire course devoted to sociological research. For this discussion, we will only touch the surface of literature review. At a graduate level, like most people, I wrote a lengthy thesis project. Thankfully, literature review has evolved in terms of tools available and ease of acquisition of materials. If you happen to have stumbled upon this book as part of a higher education or college level assignment, indeed that login code and password the institution issued for searching literature, article, and media databases will absolutely become a prized treasure. Visit your school's library.

Database Search Engine Tools

Many university libraries even offer introductory sessions or tutorials on getting started. Each search engine differs in features, functions, and operations. However, I can share some key principles to provide a glimpse of what to discover during the library's tutorial. Consider the following:

- Which field of literature would prove most helpful: Education, Technology, Social Studies, Engineering, etc.? Many of the database search engine tools start by having you select the databases to search through. If you pick too many, then the results given from the search may prove abundantly burdensome. However, selecting too few might produce little, if any, results. I recommend testing it out. Pick two or three databases such as Education and Technology, then continue to the next step of the search. If the results end up being too few, simply backtrack (usually just arrow back) until reaching the database selection page again. Hopefully, after several attempts, the correct number of databases combined with the right fields selected will provide amazing results, a list of viable scholarly articles that relate to your research topic.

- After deciding on which databases to pursue for the search, next type in a major key word or words that reflect the overall subject in question, such as "Butterflies." Type this into the first search line.

- Before hitting the "Go" or "Submit" or "Accept" button, consider adding a secondary search criterion. Perhaps the butterflies of interest must reside in California. So, in such case you would type in "California" on the secondary search line.

- Wait a second! Often students eagerly press "Go" too soon. Depending on the search tool in use, you may need to add a join feature. The join options presented normally include "and" or "or." In the case of our Butterflies in California, the "and" option would produce the best results. If we accidentally set the join to "or" the results would go on and on for pages. The system would interpret an "or" as meaning provide information about "butterflies" or "California."

- Often these sophisticated search engines will allow for multiple secondary search lines. If the butterflies of interest could reside in California or Mexico, follow the directions provided by your educational institution and set it up to search for ("California" or "Mexico") and "Butterflies". This step will vary greatly depending on the system.

Wisely Use What's Available

Even though the search engines do well in providing references to articles and other publications, remember to also make use of the simpler options. At the time of writing this book, search engines such as Google and other web-based browser services can provide helpful results. However, given the leniency of materials accepted on the World Wide Web, a careful researcher must stay accountable and only use reputable sources. Fake news and invalid claims do emerge in online platforms daily. Ideally, repeated ideas or facts expressed in unison by different experts provide a more solid input into a research study.

Stay mindful of the authored date. When did the writer put together the article or web page? In many a research, experts consider the current or recent resources more valid. The exception to the "most current five year" rule of thumb comes into play when discussing the history of a given subject. If the written report includes the origin of a given field of study, then certainly, older documentation offers acceptable mention.

Making Connections with Experts

Look back at your brain dump. Solidify topics or points to research. Consider the following tips in conducting research either through web browsers or database search engines:

- Do you have questions about the subject? Search for answers.

- Do you already have beliefs about the subject? Search for the belief you carry. Do any experts go along with your views?

- Who would care most about this subject? Search for the subject plus this person or group of people. (It would end up being an "and" join search.)

- Ideally, look for views from opposite positions, those agreeing and disagreeing on a given viewpoint.

Take time to jot down some getting started notes in your journal. It helps to organize your thoughts.

Journal Entry – (Today's Date) Questions about the subject

Journal Entry – (Today's Date) What I believe about it

Journal Entry – (Today's Date) Who agrees with my belief? Why?

Journal Entry – (Today's Date) Who disagrees? Why?

Processing Findings

While exploring and reading through the articles and various items, as you listen to podcasts, or watch videos, do so attentively. Which portions best align with your topic? Sometimes, including an interesting quote or even a paraphrase will nicely help readers understand. Make a note about any interesting quotes. Remember to also save the link or location to where you found the source. Some writers follow the style of reading, finding, then immediately writing thoughts about the point discovered. Others prefer to continue in a search mode, locate all prime sources, read, or scan, then save the materials. I do lean more towards the latter option, given that my mental processes work seemingly different in searching mode than in a writing one. Do you have enough sources?

Journal Entry – (Today's Date) Interesting quotes & sources

Beef up your arguments by including statistics. In locating good statistics, consider valid and convincing studies. Afterall, a research study that included polling 2,000 people weighs heavier than one that only took into consideration the thoughts of 20 individuals. The validity of data, though beyond the scope of this book, might prove an interesting topic to read about. As you locate multiple sources, develop a way to organize them.

If the project has great significance, then create a digital or physical folder to save findings and materials. Rename the files to best represent the findings. Often, downloading materials will yield files that have very cryptic and unintelligible names assigned by default. Renaming the digital files helps me better identify and locate them later. I use my computer mouse and right click on the file name and choose the rename option.

Artificial Intelligence

As I prepare to publish this book, artificial intelligence has emerged on scene, offering promising assistance for research writing. I just tested using ChatGpt. I keyed in "Please share top 10 spots to visit along the coast of California. Please also share the references for tracking down this information." This AI tool quickly came back with 10 vacation spots to consider and provided reference links. As a student, you will enjoy using this tool too! Double check to ensure your teacher or professor approves of the use of artificial intelligent tools. I believe the field of education does welcome the use provided students adhere to the school's guidelines. This chapter on report writing seeks to introduce you to various aspects to get you started. However, report writing entails so much more. I hope to add additional details to upcoming books. For now, I hope the information you read here will serve to get you started. How do you feel about the use of AI in today's classroom settings? How do you feel about using such tools in researching and writing papers? Record your thoughts in your journal.

Journal Entry – (Today's Date) The Rise of AI

Drafting the Report

The overall writing of report paragraphs happens in a way like that of a simple five paragraph essay – opinion or argumentative. Most reports begin with an introduction that highlights the top-level items up for discussion. If you did a mind map approach for a brain dump earlier, then the introduction could point to the main overall branches that shot out from the center topic. Each of the main branches could lead to separate body paragraphs. Most likely you may have more than three sub-branches. Therefore, the report should have more body paragraphs.

Due to the increasing number of items to discuss in a report, I often advocate switching to an outline mode for structuring the report's order. Thought maps and outlining both prove useful during the planning stage. However, a student short on time might find creating an outline more fluid, especially after an initial solo brain dump or a group brainstorming session. Research reports help scholars and society gain understanding about a wide range of testable or observable occurrences.

Special Research Reports

Scholarly reports, such as those found in a scientific or professional journal, will often require experimentation, testing, or surveying respondents. The following briefly introduces some of the key sections found in preparing such a report. Each professional field varies, so do consult with those leading the research to verify which sections will prove most meaningful or useful.

Abstract

When writing a research report, the formatting looks slightly different. Many scholarly research articles begin with an abstract section. An abstract normally contains one long paragraph summarizing the overall research and the key conclusion.

Introduction

Next, an introductory paragraph follows, much like that found in a normal essay. (See the earlier details as found in the Essay Writing chapter.)

Literature Review

The subsequent section may include an entire write up on literature review. This differs slightly from the literature review discussed earlier in this chapter. For example, in preparing for an argumentative essay, most scholars do perform a literature review. However, they do not necessarily present everything found there. They simply use the most appropriate references to prove their points. However, with a research style report, most agree it is best to report all the literature findings -- those supporting and those not supporting the research hypothesis. Within such a section, multiple paragraphs present what researchers and others have already studied, their hypotheses, discoveries, and findings.

Methods

Once the writer has included, the abstract, the introduction, and the literature review, the report presents the researcher's case. This includes stating a proposed hypothesis, which the research will take into consideration. The researcher will also describe his test population, the process for conducting the research test, and any other conditions important to the study.

Often, overall notes regarding the conducting of any survey, testing, experiments, etc. go under a methods section. In this section, the researcher reports on how he, she, or the research team carried out the study. This section could include just a few paragraphs or several depending on the complexities of the research.

Results

Finally, the researcher will share the findings and the results of the research study. A good researcher will also disclose any bias that may be present in the data. Did the study conclude as expected? Most will end this section by sharing the results of the tested hypothesis. Did the test turn out as planned?

Discussion

As a wrap up, the research will recap the initial thesis, share overall findings, and propose a call to action – what should happen next? Should experts conduct further research? Should funding for special programs get approved?

The actual sequencing of the paragraphs does vary. If writing a research paper for fulfilling a class assignment, follow the template requirements as presented by the teacher or professor. Most likely the content will consist of what this chapter has already mentioned. However, the ordering of the materials can and do vary greatly. Many reports serve to inform a community about options. We have considered research reporting. An informational reporting style often appears in magazines, newspapers, and other literature that a casual reader might pick up.

If your environment supports conducting a research type of report, proceed with planning out your research study, conducting it, then write the report. Use this next journal to jot down notes about your plan. If your environment does not support conducting research, then use your imagination. If given the opportunity, what type of research would fascinate you most. Journal your thoughts.

Journal Entry – (Today's Date) My Research Study

Informational Reports

Informational Reports do not contain the same complexities as a research report. The planning steps look much like that used in writing a five-paragraph essay, only the writer ends up with more than five.

For example, if we shared the top ten restaurants to visit while in Rome, this type of report would most likely include 12 paragraphs. One for the introduction, one for each of the ten restaurants, and an overall summary would total up to twelve paragraphs. Follow the same pattern as used when writing a five-paragraph essay but adjust the thesis statement. You would not necessarily list out all ten restaurants in the thesis. Rather, you might note, the number ten. "10 restaurants in Rome won the award for excellence and each delighted the taste buds of the judges." The other components of the introduction remain the same as those of a regular essay.

Challenge yourself! You have just been asked to advise readers on how to go about selecting the best pen, car, dress, shoes, or something else. Report on the top five. Use the next journal entry to organize your thoughts.

Journal Entry – (Today's Date) The Top Five

Summary

Developing excellence in writing and formatting reports takes patience, practice, and time. Combining your own brain dump knowledge on a subject of interest with the ideas and expertise of others – gained through brainstorming or database searches -- will result in a better outcome. Carefully conducting a literature review will save time in the long run and produce some keen insights. Reports vary greatly in terms of their content and sequencing. Planning and thoughtfully sequencing your report will help you stand out as a more professional writer.

Chapter Questions

1. Having a limited understanding about a topic should not stop or hinder you from engaging in report writing. Do you agree? Explain.

2. Compare and contrast brain dump and brainstorming as discussed in this chapter. In what ways have you already found these approaches helpful? How do you hope to use brain dumps and brainstorming in the future?

3. You have been appointed to facilitate a camping type trip, a retreat for a group of 12 people. These campers have signed up for a "Writing in the Woods" day. Walk yourself through a brain dump. How would you prepare for this trip?

4. You decided to gather three people plus yourself to brainstorm some ideas for the trip or retreat mentioned above. You need to produce some sort of guide booklet to pass out to those attending the trip. How would you conduct the meeting? You serve as the brainstorming initiator.

5. What could you use instead of a formal university library database search tool?

6. Explain the usefulness of a literature review.

7. How do you plan on organizing sources and materials for your reports?

8. Which method do you think works best when planning a report: thought mapping, outlining, or something else? Explain.

Professionally speaking,

stealing ideas or words from others

counts as plagiarism.

Chapter 15 Writing Standards and Styles

Chapter Objectives

- Gain an understanding of why writers adhere to standards.

- Practice writing a paper using the MLA standard style.

- Explore MLA resources found on Purdue University's website.

- Use the Citation Machine to aid in creating the "Works Cited" page and the intext citations.

- Inspect a sample MLA style paper, paying attention to formatting standards.

- Experiment with MLA templates commonly found in popular word processing software applications. Such templates simplify MLA formatting.

- Define plagiarism and understand harmful pitfalls.

When writing daily and simply conveying your personal viewpoints, teachers and professors may extend leniency in terms of overall formatting and presentation of content. However, education platforms, institutes, schools, colleges, universities, and higher education have accelerated the demand for submitting a more professional paper. Thus, many such scholarly locations will require adherence to formal standards. Given such an increasing need to follow such standards, in reviewing and editing this book, I felt it important to add in a chapter to help you get started in writing in a standardized fashion.

The Style Challenge

In thinking about this topic, my mind wrestles with change. Writing standards change regularly, making it difficult to even prescribe a certain set of rules for you to learn. Accordingly, we will set out to discover how to find the most current set of standards for a given field of study. For this book's consideration, we will primarily focus on the MLA Standards and associated style of writing. I am refraining from including screenshots or pictures of menus since changes do occur routinely. Instead, I describe where to find or look at the current style and the rules or standards. Please note that this chapter serves to give you a nice introduction and does not include everything.

Purdue University

At the time of writing this book, Purdue University has a well-known reputation for housing the most relevant and current information on writing standards.[9] Many scholars and writers refer to Purdue's writing

---

[9] (The OWL at Purdue 2022)

tools as a wise OWL. So, think "**Purdue OWL**" and type that into your internet search browser. To add preciseness to your search, please also add in "**MLA**" as the style. Search the internet for "**Purdue OWL MLA**." You should readily find the current URL links that lead to the resources needed to continue our discussion. Click on the link for the "**MLA Formatting and Style Guide**." Yes, you will notice many ads. The sponsors of the ads help to pay for the OWL tools. Just X out of these if they cover up important information on the display. Periodically, you may receive a prompt for a paid subscription plan or an invitation to watch a commercial to continue using the tools. I normally just watch their commercials though given the frequency of my using these tools maybe a subscription would make sense.

Sample Paper

We will explore the basics of the MLA standards. Feel free to read more outside of our discussions. Locate the MLA Formatting and Style Guide topic list. On my screen, I see it positioned on the left. Scroll down and find "MLA Sample Paper." Study this paper to gain familiarity with the standards.

After briefly reviewing the sample MLA paper, take a few minutes to write some observations in your journal. What benefits come by following a certain format such as that used with the MLA style?

Journal Entry – (Today's Date) Benefits of Standards

Next, I would like to point out some key things to keep in mind as you continue learning how to write using the MLA style.

Heading

Pay attention to the heading layout of the paper. Most software applications just require you to double click in the top portion of the display window to prepare for entering header content. Notice the last name of the student writer along with a page number appears at the top right corner. By placing text such as your name and page number in the header section, this would result in your info repeating on subsequent pages. Your software should have an insert page number option. This will allow the page numbers to increase automatically.

Details about the student and professor names along with the course and date appear double spaced on the left and positioned outside of the header. Make sure to click outside of the header section before typing this part in. You do not want it to repeat on multiple pages. Pay attention to the formatting style of the date. See the sample paper to gain clarity. These items do not repeat on subsequent pages, thus make sure not to put them in the header section in your word processing document.

Take a few minutes to practice just the first part of setting up an MLA paper. See if you could position your last name and the page number in the header section. See if you could get other information about your name, teacher or professor, the class identification, and the date to go outside of the header section. Use the sample paper as a model but feel free to change the words to match your actual class.

For the body, you can just type in random words and letters for now to reach the second page or put in a page break in the body. Did your header automatically appear on the second page? It should only contain your last name and the page number.

After getting the header and starting information to place correctly, take a few minutes to journal about the experience and any learning observations encountered.

Journal Entry – (Today's Date) Getting started with MLA

Overall layout

The sample paper gives you a nice idea of the overall layout. Return to the OWL Purdue MLA Formatting and Style Guide and find "**MLA General Format**." Currently, the general overall formatting recommends using a Times New Roman font with a point size of 12. Letter size paper (8 ½" x 11") has long been an MLA standard. Notice the required margins of 1" all the way around – top, bottom, left, and right. Set the MLA line spacing to double with zero amount of before and after paragraph spacing indicated. This style permits using only one space after the end of sentence period. (In years gone by, everyone pressed space two times between each sentence.)

Since each paragraph will start with a .5 or ½" indent, I recommend configuring this in your overall document settings. Depending on the software used, the location of this setting could appear under a formatting menu as alignment. Instead of having to press tab for each paragraph, consider using a ½" first line indent. (Depending on your software, this may reside under a special option for alignment and indentations.)

MLA Templates

Some writing software systems include MLA templates in their complimentary selections. Check the directions for your given software to see if this option exists for you. Microsoft Word and Google Docs both currently have such resources available.[10], [11] These templates already have the margins, the fonts, and basic setups in place. You will simply type over their mockup text. Such text temporarily holds the positions, so you know where to type.

Please check with your instructor or professor if you do your work on a school device such as a laptop or tablet. Some institutions do not include all the templates by default. So, if you see a list of templates and the MLA one does not show up in the list, please double check with your school to see if they permit using it. It might have just been skipped in their setup of the equipment, or teachers and professors may have purposefully decided to have students position everything in their documents without the aid of such a easy to use template.

---

[10] (Microsoft 2022)
[11] (Google n.d.)

Say "No" to Plagiarism

Obviously, well, maybe not so obvious – Yes, you must do your own work! As you advance to new levels, perhaps going for a high school honors status, or climbing higher to complete a college bachelor's degree program, or even higher to achieve a master's or doctorate level, stay honest. Do you realize that copying someone else's work without giving them any credit for the words written will flag you as dishonest and potentially harm your future? I do wish discussing this topic did not warrant any mention in this book. However, having witnessed students entangled by the perils of plagiarism, I feel it a responsible action on my part to warn you.

If you find information on the internet and copy it for your essay or report, that counts as plagiarism. If you read something on the internet, then simply put it in your own words for your report, that still counts as plagiarism. In both cases, to escape such a situation, you must give credit to the author of the content even if you choose to use your own words. Professionally speaking, stealing ideas or words from others counts as plagiarism. Oh, and at the time of my writing this book, people advertise online services in which they will write your essay for you. Do not fall into such a trap. As an educator, I have quickly detected that a student made use of such services. Keep your honesty intact! Allow plenty of time on your schedule to prepare a nice essay, one that you will feel a great sense of accomplishment on completion.

The penalty of plagiarism varies considerably among different institutions. Most schools and educational organizations do not take plagiarism lightly and will often state in writing, inside of their admissions literature, their policy should a student be even suspected of committing such a crime. Plagiarism in some cases could result in the loss of a chance to graduate from an educational institution. On the outskirts, this may sound rather harsh. However, at a higher level of schooling, these organizations expect students to already come in knowing right from wrong and comprehending the seriousness of writing thievery. So, they discipline accordingly. At the very least, students' grades suffer along with their reputations. Should you find yourself tempted to fail in this area, please get help! Do not risk your future on such a poor decision. Take some time to ponder the ramifications of plagiarism. In your journal, record your thoughts.

Journal Entry – (Today's Date) The Dangers of Plagiarism

In working with students from many different cultural backgrounds, often I hear, "I did not even know." In such a case, if this applies to you, keep reading as we consider how to give credit where credit is due.

Works Cited

As shared earlier, we live in an age in which many forms of information exist. Articles, journals, newspapers, videos, movies, interviews, artistic pieces, radio broadcasts, television shows, social and media posts all contain bits of information. You gain intelligence, information for your essays and reports, and in doing so, writing standards require that your paper includes a disclosure on where you obtained such knowledge. Take a moment and look at the Sample Works Cited page located on the Purdue OWL MLA Formatting and Style Guide website. Do you see the sample provided? Next, we will briefly assess how to construct the Works Cited page. This goes at the end of your MLA essay or report.

Consider the Source

You must cite each source. Each article, media, webpage, and so forth make up a source. Your essay will most likely have multiple sources. Often a solid essay does have many sources to help prove and add integrity to the written paper and its author. So, the first step in preparing the works cited page has to do with personal assessment. Go through and make a list or take notes as to which sources you will use in writing the essay. You will want to include a citation entry for each of these. Please keep in mind that each one of your references (sources) comes with differing levels of trust, credibility, and authority. For example, if your essay seeks to provide insights into pollution in the ocean, citing a meaningful study conducted by a group of oceanographers would weigh heavier than that written by a group of random people taking a trip to the coffee shop.

Additionally, more advancements occur with the passing of time, thus articles written within the last five years often gain an increased recognition over older ones. Historical reporting would prove an exception as older articles would add purpose to such cases. Carefully consider the publish date of the sources you use and who wrote them.

Consider the Formatting

The entries for an MLA Works Cited page vary depending on the type of source used. For example, a newspaper source entry looks different than an online web page source entry. Thankfully, the Purdue

University OWL MLA Formatting and Style Guide along with the Citation Machine will both prove helpful resources when the time comes for creating the citation entries. Follow the steps provided here to get started using these tools.

Find the URL or Copyright Information

Many students obtain information from the World Wide Web. When you find meaningful articles and other media online, make sure to copy down the URL. I find it most helpful to keep a running list of these URLs by copying/pasting them into a temporary document of sorts. Save these URLs for the Purdue OWL Citation Machine step.

If you use information from a book or other source not found on the internet, turn past the inside cover, and locate the copyright page. This normally appears after the title page. If you are temporarily borrowing this source, consider photocopying or taking a picture of this page. Keep these in a folder and have them ready for the Purdue OWL Citation Machine step.

Return to the Purdue OWL MLA Formatting and Style Guide web page. Find their listing of MLA topics (most likely positioned on the left). Do you see all the "MLA Works Cited" options? Select the one that best describes your source type. If you found your information on a website, then select "MLA Works Cited: Electronic Sources." After making your selection, carefully review the information located on the right side of the page. This will explain the requirements for creating the citation entry. Before you begin to panic, I have good news! The Citation Machine available from the Purdue OWL site will do much of the work for you. This information that you see now on the Purdue OWL site will become useful when proofreading. The Citation Machine does not always get everything right. Return here to double check the formatting. Look at OWL notes to see if comma, periods, and quotation marks land in the correct places. Also, pay close attention to upper-and lower-case lettering requirements and to italics.

I recommend returning to this site annually as you write future papers. The style rules for MLA change over time. Purdue University does a great job at maintaining their website and making such style updates known. Proceed onward to the discussion of the Citation Machine.

Are you ready to create your first citation? Find an article on the internet to use for practicing this next portion.

Citation Machine

Towards the top right-hand side of the Purdue University OWL MLA Formatting and Style Guide, notice "Cite your source automatically in MLA." Do you see the small pull-down selection arrow? It wants you to select where you got your information. Most of the time students choose, "Website." Make your choice. The Citation Machine designed by Chegg Inc, embedded as a tool inside of the OWL site will help you create your citations.[12]

Next, if you have a URL, copy/paste it into the provide blank. If the source resides outside of the internet, follow the instructions located just inside of the blank, such as searching by book title. You would type in the title of the book. Now, click the "**Cite**" button. Follow the onscreen instructions to complete the creation of the citation entry. Make sure to check carefully and verify all the fill-in blanks that appear along the way. Remember, the Citation Machine, as a digital tool, does not always detect graphically displayed information. In such cases, manually fill in the blanks with the correct data.

---

[12] (Chegg 2003-2022)

Tip: In a separate web browser tab or window, bring up the actual webpage being cited. Keep the Purdue OWL and Citation Machine open in a separate window or tab. Go back and forth between the fill-in the blank Citation Machine page and the actual webpage being cited. Carefully proof each field for correctness. Often, some data may not even be available. Keep in mind that placing this citation entry into the works cited section will help the reader know how to locate this information. Do you have enough details filled in the blanks to provide the readers with a roadmap so they can find and read the source article or other media?

Most scholars do not frown on minor missing entries, especially if the originator of the source did not make them available. However, if you happen to find yourself on such an adventure at a doctoral or upper degree level, do consult with your professor or academic advisor. Some experts in academia require the student to completely throw out and not include anything from a source that has missing citation pieces. Remember, if you do end up throwing out such a source, the matching written content in your essay or report must be eliminated to avoid plagiarism accusations. Once you have finished filling in as many blanks as possible, follow the instructions on the screen to accept the entries.

You should then receive the fully formatted citation for your source. You may now copy this onto your Works Cited page located at the end of your essay or report.

A Special Word About Formatting the Citation Entry

Look at the sample Works Cited page provided on the Purdue site. Notice the need to adhere to the same general formatting as relevant to the rest of the paper: Times New Roman, 12 point, and double spaced. Notice the appearance of the text. Do you see the first line of each entry hangs out over the rest? This is called a "hanging indent." To format in this manner, highlight the citation entries, search under the formatting menu option for the word processing software in use, such as Word or Google Docs, and look for the alignment or indentation selection, then most likely you will see a special option for setting a hanging indent. Set the hanging indent to ½ inch (.5"). Alternatively, you may manually set this using the little ruler controls located just above the document. Once you have finished creating all citation entries, make sure to alphabetize and reorder them as appropriate.

The Matching Game – In Text Citations

Congratulations on completing the Works Cited Page or at least having begun to understand the process. However, a dilemma exists. How will the reader know which parts of your essay or report apply to the citations found on the works cited page? For that answer, we turn our attention to **intext citations.**

If you have already tested out using the Citation Machine, a citation entry and an intext entry appeared in a highlighted green area. If you do not see the intext entry, but do see the citation one, simply hover your mouse over the citation entry and look for a clickable intext entry option. Click on that option.

For better understanding in-text citations, direct your attention back to the OWL Purdue MLA Formatting Guide. Look again at the topic list on the left side of the screen. Find and select the one listed as "**MLA In-Text Citations: The Basics.**"

On the right side of the screen, helpful formatting guidelines display examples of how the in-text citation works and looks. For each entry listed on your works cited page, go through, and include an in-text citation. For each entry, first start by finding the location in the body portion of your essay or report in which you wrote about the details being cited. Next, return to OWL Purdue's formatting guide, select "MLA in-text Citation: The Basics" from the list on the left of the screen display. Scroll through the right side of the examples found on the screen, locating the one that best matches your actual situation. Follow the example given for formatting your in-text citation.

Once you have included the in-text citation, readers will easily have a way to match this portion of your essay with the works cited entries located at the end.

Summary

Writing standards routinely change. Become comfortable with accessing Purdue University's writing style resources to stay updated. Authenticity in writing adds to character and professionalism. Anything less puts one at risk of losing trust and not achieving academic goals. Modern templates allow writers to comply with standards more readily. As your writing matures and you follow standards, people view your work in a more professional light.

Chapter Questions

1. Why do writers follow standards such as MLA?

2. Practice writing an essay or report that requires the inclusion of quotes or paraphrasing of thoughts from one or more sources. Make sure to include both intext citations and the Works Cited page. You can also use an MLA writing template.

3. Explain the resources that Purdue University has MLA standards.

4. Use the Citation Machine to aid in creating a Works Cited page. Share your experience. How did the tool help?

5. Share at least five requirements for writing in an MLA format.

6. What is plagiarism? Why should writers not plagiarize?

Section 7: The Finale

Before concluding this book, I want to challenge you to reassess your personal sweet spot. This section gives you an opportunity to put the pieces together. We will revisit various chapters, especially those found in Section 2: Identity. In this concluding section, I challenge you to practice presenting yourself to other people. As discussed earlier, you will need to take all your ideas and innovations, organize them, showcase them, and communicate well. Many people feel nervous or uncomfortable about presenting. I think that stems from not really having a clear understanding of one's identity and courage to speak. This world needs more courageous people to step forward and make a difference. I believe you have what it takes to do so. Go change the world! Go make a difference. I wrote this book with such a goal in mind. I want you to boldly step forward even now. We need people like you!

Understanding the culture of an organization, interacting with the rest of the team, being mindful of wider or broader needs across the corporation, takes time and commitment.

Chapter 16 Presenting You!

Chapter Objectives

- Circle back around to clarify your personal strengths and sweet spot.

- Take the challenge to organize and update your portfolio.

- Discuss the importance of individual character and presentation.

- Articulate the power of a solid team.

- Practice organizing thoughts and connecting ideas together.

- Commit to innovation and professional writing.

We have covered much ground: journaling, narrative writing, sentence structure, personal discovery, portfolio development, note taking, study skills, word power, vocabulary development, critical thinking, essay writing, report preparation, and MLA standards. As a recap, and to address the matter of presenting yourself to others, in this final chapter pull together all the various pieces that represent you and clearly look in the mirror.

Getting to Know You

Repeatedly throughout life, as the clock ticks, various types of people will seek to know you. In some situations, you, the presenter may not need to display very much at all, especially if everyone gathered in the room already knows each other. However, quite often, and not surprisingly, other individuals listen and watch you more intently. They have key decisions on their plate and set out to size up your potential and assess a possible match with their future opportunities. Such opportunities may include acceptance into a university, the awarding of a scholarship or grant, permission to borrow a significant sum of money to launch a business, or the filling of an opening in a new career position. If working for yourself or a family business, this "getting to know you" may come in the form of potential new clients assessing if your business might meet their needs. Can they trust you and your organization to provide the best products or services? In any case, presenting yourself does deserve ink on the page and warrants our attention in this closing section.

The Team

I try not to look back in time too much, for some report it as a sign of aging. I want to stay young, at least in mind and heart! However, as my eyes read through the pages already written here, memories dear to my heart flood so deeply that I cannot help but pause to include a smile and mention here. A spot on our team seldom came up, at least not for a permanent position. The reason had to do with the kinship and family spirit that ran through and knitted us all together. Also, each person selected proved talented.

I took the adding of a team member to our already solidified group seriously. Yes, the interviewing process did take on a weighty tone. For the most part, a new hire, someone just added, would require at least a year's investment before fully acclimating into the team and being able to function well. Sure, newcomers would prove a great asset from the start. However, as they receive training and work alongside other colleagues, they would not only learn mind challenging kinds of things but also grow culturally. Understanding the culture of an organization, interacting with the rest of the team, being mindful of wider or broader needs across the corporation, takes time and commitment. So, in reviewing applications of newcomers interested in joining our team, I looked for stability.

If I saw time gaps on a resume, unless a cover letter or some sort of communication sufficiently explained the in between segments, seldom would I seriously consider hiring the person. Why? Investing in a person and seeing the team grow to accept such an individual really deserves a sense of loyalty and trust, a sense of commitment. As you prepare for future presentations of your own qualifications, be sure to share your

heart -- your character and conduct. Can people rely on you? Do you

take responsibility? Could you work both in a team and independently?

Journal your thoughts.

Journal Entry – (Today's Date) Team or Independent Work

Organization of Thought

Yes, pick up your journaling book or digital journaling entries again.

Thumb through the pages and files and take time to assess how you

have structured or unraveled your inward thoughts. Look at all the

insights you wrote about. How have you organized the observations and

thoughts made about your environment, your hopes, and dreams? No

doubt, such ordering has developed through practice. Has your writing

taken on new levels of detail?

Continue the journaling and writing of life thoughts. This diligence,

now part of your routine, your habits so to speak, shows promise. Such

careful attention should not be given lightly. Be encouraged to continue

writing and shape, mold, and fit such ordering to best work with your

character, personality, and manner of thinking. Especially practice

putting your thoughts and approaches to life into words, and do so in a way that speaks to your heart, mind, and soul. Do you plan to continue journaling? Write your thoughts.

Journal Entry – (Today's Date) My Writing Future

Connecting Ideas Together

The ability to relate topics and ideas together will lend nicely to the already discussed skill of organizing thoughts. Towards the beginning of this book, you journaled about environmental sounds. Additionally, you learned how to include other senses. By recording and connecting your observations regarding all five senses, the descriptions became clearer and more precise.

Later, I challenged you to imagine adding one or more characters and to create a narrative. By connecting sensory thoughts about the environment and adding in such creative usage, this beautiful tapestry allows you to engage in an innovative manner. You created something new!

Pause now, and reflect on how you personally create original thoughts, new ideas, and even unique stories. This too will benefit you personally, and it will spark innovation that any organization that might choose to employ your services would desire. I challenge you to put into words the steps personally taken during this journey. Can you share such a process with someone else? How have you grown and developed? Do any parts need revisiting?

Journal Entry – (Today's Date) My Growth and Development

Creativity and Innovation

Hopefully by now, you enjoy creating new ideas, thoughts, narratives, and experiencing innovations as much as I do. Make sure to let your listeners know that you like innovation. You like being a part of groups and organizations that allow you the opportunity to create. You enjoy using creativity in a productive manner. Imagine stepping into an environment where the leaders approach you, expressing a hunger for newness in their organization. Can they find such a unique mindset? Does it make sense for you to join the team, the group, or company? Practice innovation! It will most certainly come up for discussion!

Sweet Spot

As we are preparing to close this book, I must ask again, what do you enjoy? What skills do you possess? In which high demand areas could you best use your talents? In meeting with future leaders, prospective university admissions counselors, and potential employers, the ability to properly communicate your sweet spot will serve as an asset. It will help to place you in the best matched positions. How comfortable do you feel about communicating your sweet spot?

Journal Entry – (Today's Date) Communicating Sweet Spot

Convincing and Professional Writing

By now, the importance of developing writing skills and putting your best foot forward has solidified. With every school assignment and each writing opportunity outside of campus, make sure to do your best. Double check your work, beef up vocabulary, add in adjectives and adverbs, include senses, and pay attention to the 5Ws – where, when, who, what, and why. Adding a suspenseful plot, full of rising actions, a good guy, and a bad guy will serve as icing on the cake. Refine your fiction writing without forgetting to also work on the nonfiction side of the fence.

Build Your Portfolio

Hopefully, you have added to your personal portfolio along the way. It now contains essays, reports, narrative writings, picture albums, and written thoughts that represent yourself to others. Take time to reflect on the journey. What else can you include in your portfolio? I encourage

you to take time even now to update and add to it. Jot down notes as
you plan.

Journal Entry – (Today's Date) Building My Portfolio

Portfolio Presentation

Continue adding to your personal portfolio, adjusting, and changing
it along the way. As noted earlier, in this digital age, portfolios serve as
your calling card. It provides a means for other people to get better
acquainted with you. Even so, I must offer one word of caution. Do not
think that the portfolio alone can best represent you. Rather, if given the
opportunity, treat it more like a slide show. Use it to walk others through
and explain key points in the process. May I suggest getting together
with other students or individuals and practice presenting your
portfolio. Share about yourself, your sweet spot, and your dreams for
the future. Have courage! Exchange helpful feedback with one another.
Write some notes about what you learned during the presentations and
feedback.

Journal Entry – (Today's Date) Presentation Insights

Summary

How do you see yourself? Contribute to our society by shining in your sweet spot and being personable. If engaging in nonfiction writing, follow recommended paragraph structures, and provide reference supports to back up your thoughts. Remember to build upon a powerful thesis statement. Most of all, enjoy the process! Also, continue developing your narrative story. Strive to see this turn into a published book! Having come this far, publishing a book certainly should rank somewhere in your bucket list. Especially, develop a winning portfolio, one that represents you in an excellent manner.

Chapter Questions

1. How does knowing your personal strengths and having examples in your portfolio help prepare you for the future?

2. What changes do you want to make to the portfolio? After listing the changes, carve out time on your schedule to do it.

3. Both working independently and as a team player stand out as vital skills. How would you rate your ability and current level in these two arenas?

4. What can you do to strengthen your abilities in working independently and as a team player?

Many leaders argue that the people skills weigh heavier in the hiring process than book knowledge.

Chapter 17 The Next Chapter of Your Life

Chapter Objectives

- Wrap up this part of our journey by highlighting some of the key concepts presented in the book.

- Set goals for the future.

- Commit to moving forward with a higher level of excellence.

We have traveled together through a whole assortment of topics pertaining to language arts and life. In this concluding chapter, take time to challenge yourself to continue developing your skills. As I summarize in this book, jot down some goals.

Business Vocabulary

We have explored different ways to improve your vocabulary. Make developing your vocabulary repertoire a routine practice. What favorite ways have you discovered to build your word power? Whichever method works the best for you, do it persistently.

Ethics, Manners, and Attentiveness

Critical thinking does require paying close attention to others and listening carefully; in doing so, no doubt patience grows. As you embark on listening more attentively to others. People will regard you as mannerly. Such care and kindness will take you far. How do you think these three fits together: careful listening, respecting others, and critical thinking? These add up to what in industry many leaders regard as excellent people skills. Leaders argue that the people skills weigh heavier in the hiring process than book knowledge. You will need both!

SQ3R and Study Skills

Practicing SQ3R and using it in deciphering textbooks will help you. Absolutely, this method does take time. However, the results impact your classwork. Upper-level classes do require more solid focus time, especially at a college level. Think about it this way; if you or I need to have a surgeon cut our bodies open to make repairs, we would want a doctor who understands well and has the expertise. Be encouraged to study deeply! Adapt methods to best fit with your needs and time allotment. However, may I warn you not to simply wing it! Have a plan and stick to it. Could you express in words how you study? Can you communicate this clearly? Take a moment and make some notes in your journal about any goals or approaches you decide to tackle in the upcoming days.

Journal Entry – (Today's Date) Goals for Studying

Self-Starter and Able to Independently Learn

Often in life, you will need to research, to explore, to learn, and to pioneer in a new field and unique areas or bodies of knowledge. Starting with a study plan approach and adding personal discipline will put you on the journey of being a self-starter or independent learner. Did you know that some people never move to this level of operation in their lives? Challenge yourself to practice taking such initiative. One key question often asked by employers has to do with this whole area. Can you work independently? Can you? Could you figure things out on your own if needed? Hopefully, our journey has helped you begin this endeavor. Think about your own process. If you need to study and learn about new things, how will you proceed? Would you do journaling, research, brain dump, apply SQ3R to reading materials, outline, or map thoughts? Take time to make notes in a journal. Can you express this in words?

Journal Entry – (Today's Date) My Approach

Team Player and Team Leader

No company desires its employees to simply stand as lone rangers. Yes, you will need to take the initiative and learn independently.

However, you also need to participate as a great team player. When each person on the team carefully does their part, when individually they bring to the table discoveries and discussions, a synergistic collaboration takes place that results in a superb outcome! Do you consider yourself a team player? Do you respect other people's input? Think about it. Can you express in words how you feel working in a group or a team? Take time to capture and journal your thoughts.

Journal Entry – (Today's Date) Teams

Presentations

Along the way, we have shared presentations and how others might view you. In addition to writing with clear thoughts, organizing each carefully, and synthesizing to create new ideas and inventions, practice presenting. Having confidence, speaking clearly, relating to your audience, and doing so with care and kindness takes practice. Think of your own approach. Do you have any goals for improving in this area? Can you express how you give presentations? Could you put this into words? Take time to record any presentation goals into your journal.

Journal Entry – (Today's Date) Presentation Goals

Moldable, Interested, and Intelligent

Standing in front of other people with the purpose of sharing about yourself, the work accomplished, and desires for the future might feel a bit intimidating. With some practice, this will get easier. Overall, you will want leaders to know of your interests. Convey your experience but also express a willingness to grow. Most companies and organizations, when interviewing, will watch, listen, and pay attention to not only the current makeup of the individuals, but growth potential. Do you see yourself as someone willing to learn? Could a leader or other team player come alongside you and give you the opportunity to learn the ropes in a new environment? Stay humble. Stay moldable. However, know your values and do not compromise in these areas. Values normally speak to ethics and morality. Provided that the training being offered does not intrude on such territory, then welcome it. Keep growing!

Conclusion

I have enjoyed crafting and designing these learning and writing adventures. Should you take all the contents, apply them to heart and mind, and because of such endeavors find this journey beneficial, then my purpose in writing this book has been quite fruitful and fulfilling. Stay in touch and let me know of your personal progress. Email addresses change over time, so feel free to search for my current one, and drop me a line. As of the writing of this book, my email address is Nancy@NBVelasco.com and my main website is NancyVelasco.com. If you search for me on the internet or book suppliers, make sure to include my middle initial, "Nancy B. Velasco." Also, if you have enjoyed this book, please give it excellent star ratings. If you have questions or think of other things to include in upcoming editions, please send me an email or message. Once again, thank you so much for joining me on this writing journey!

Bibliography

Armstrong, Patricia. 2010. *Vanderbilt University Center for Teaching.*
Accessed December 20, 2022. https://cft.vanderbilt.edu/guides-
sub-pages/blooms-taxonomy/.

Chegg. 2003-2022. *Chegg.* Accessed December 20, 2022.
https://www.chegg.com/writing/features/citation-generator.

Collins, Jim. 2001. *Good to Great.* London, England: Random House
Business Books.

Corel Corporation. n.d. *MindManager.* Accessed December 20, 2022.
https://www.mindmanager.com.

Cornell University. n.d. *Note Taking Public.* Accessed December 20,
2022. https://canvas.cornell.edu/courses/1451.

Covey, Stephen. 2020. *Seven Habits of Highly Effective People.* New York:
Simon & Schuster.

Google. n.d. *Google Docs.* Accessed December 20, 2022.
https://www.google.com/docs/about/.

LoveToKnow. 2022. *Your Dictionary.* Accessed December 20, 2022.
https://www.yourdictionary.com.

Microsoft. 2022. *MIcrosoft 365.* Accessed December 20, 2022.

https://www.microsoft.com/en-us/microsoft-365?rtc=1.

Robinson, Francis P. 1946. *Effective Study.* New York: Harper & Brothers.

TED Conference, LLC. n.d. *TED Ideas Worth Spreading.* Accessed

December 20, 2022. https://www.ted.com.

The OWL at Purdue. 2022. *Purdue OWL College of Liberal Arts.* Accessed

December 20, 2022. https://owl.purdue.edu/.

Vocabulary.com, a Division of IXL Learning. 2022. *Vocabulary.com.*

Accessed December 20, 2022. https://www.vocabulary.com.

Author Biography

Nancy B. Velasco, MSEd. has her master's degree in education with an emphasis in Online Instruction. After completing her undergraduate degree, Ms. Velasco taught and led in post-secondary (adult) schools for over 11 years. During this time, she wrote her first book in computer technology. It got published when computer networking started becoming popular. She taught a variety of subjects at the time, mostly computer, business, and keyboarding.

She went on to lead a small technology team in a midsize Christian credit union. In this role the team supported the desktop, laptop, and phone infrastructure for the organization. Nancy B. Velasco facilitated Technology Training, sharing bits and pieces of "how to's" for the enterprise staffing. Nancy's team also led significant technology projects. After 16 years working at the credit union, Ms. Velasco left to help at a church in the community.

Nancy enjoyed helping in multiple ways, though her official title read Church Administrator or Secretary. She led in children's church, facilitated Bible studies, counseled women one-on-one, and did intercessory prayer. Nancy did many behind the scenes duties: computer repair, media setup, spreadsheets, database management, and life group administration support. She also published her first inspirational book, Untangled Spirit and Unfrozen Heart. Nancy began tutoring students after school. She eventually left the church administration role and began private tutoring full-time.

Velasco offers private and group help in English language communications. Current focus primarily centers around helping clients and their families develop writing, reading, vocabulary, spelling, and presentation skills. Several have expressed experiencing higher grades in school. Some have gone on to write their own books. In addition to partnering with individuals in a mentoring or coaching fashion, Ms. Velasco has written and published over 20 books. She writes inspirational spiritual books, children's story books, and educational instructions. Nancy still enjoys tutoring online and seeks to introduce educational books and resources to help even more students.